JUST DECIDE

JUST DECIDE

Fail-Proof Strategies to Up-Level
Your Life, Career, and Relationships

For more information, email *justdecidecoach@gmail.com*

ISBN: 978-1-7329538-4-0

Cover design: Julie Shatovayulia
(Instagram @shatovayuliya)

Interior Design: Lazar Kackarovski

JUST DECIDE

FAIL-PROOF STRATEGIES TO UP-LEVEL YOUR LIFE, CAREER, AND RELATIONSHIPS

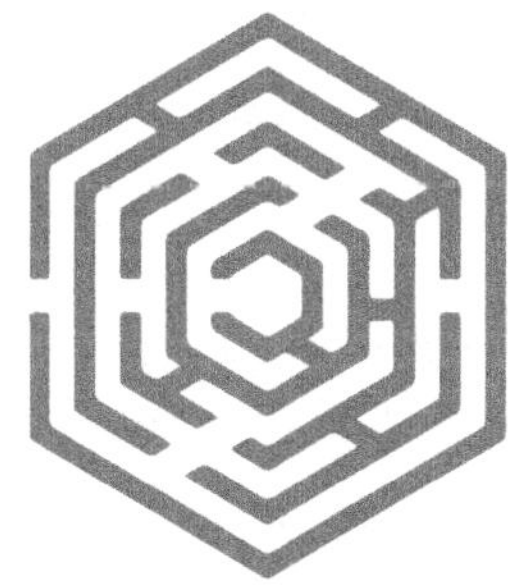

by

TSGOYNA TANZMAN,

M.A./CCC SLP

Certified Life Coach/Master Practitioner NLP

READ THIS FIRST

Thanks for deciding to begin your journey!

GRAB YOUR FREE GIFT!

Readers have the most success when they use the interactive workbook.

- Decide the life you want
- Clarify your intentions
- Take massive action

ARE YOU READY?

Download your FREE WORKBOOK

https://bit.ly/3Bxzllz

ACKNOWLEDGMENTS

The work and ideas presented in this book are based upon the teachings, trainings, thousands of hours of study, certifications, personal self-development, and client coaching sessions I've experienced with the most influential thought leaders of our time. The result is a mix of science, metaphysics, spirituality, and humor.

I've been a personal self-development enthusiast since I was four years old. I remember listening to the story *The Little Engine That Could* by Watty Piper and feeling the optimism and excitement of the little engine's refrain: "I think I can, I think I can." At that tender age, I identified with the engine who nobody thought was special, who didn't have the fancy engine or parlor or dining cars, who didn't have the size and strength of the others, but who had the desire to help save the day and bring toys to the children who were waiting for them. That desire to serve gave her the courage to say, "I think I can," even though she had no evidence she could possibly help. Listening to that refrain as she huffed up the mountain thrilled me with the belief that things were possible because you *thought* them to be. There were no genies or magic wands or fairy godmothers that created a magical outcome; it was just a simple engine that *thought* she could do something and committed to doing it. This is the basic principle Tony Robbins talks about when he says, "Your destiny depends on three things: what you focus on, what you make it mean, and what you do about it."

I am grateful for the teachings and trainings of the many beloved authors and thought leaders with whom I've studied, trained, and obtained certifications, including Tony Robbins, Brooke Castillo, Derek Rydall, Richard Bandler, Dawson Church, Eckhart Tolle, and Esther and Abraham Hicks. While each of these teachers is a legend in the field of personal development and has dedicated their lives to sharing revolutionary, nuanced ideas, analogies, personal stories, and examples, their teachings all return to the core simplicity and universal truth that *our thoughts affect our outcomes*. This was the spiritual teaching of *The Little Engine That Could.*

A special shout of love and appreciation for my husband, Paul, who has supported and loved me through the worst and the best of thirty-five years of marriage. Our soul contract keeps me growing and flourishing in unexpected ways.

I want to thank the many women who supported me during this project and vulnerably shared their "Just Decide" stories for the moments in their lives where they shifted their thoughts and took empowered actions. First, to my courageous sister, Leslie, who "cheated death twice" and instead decided how she wanted to live. To the indomitable Sage, who is perhaps the most determined and resilient woman I know, who recovered from a serious stroke that required demanding rehabilitation and relearned how to walk, talk, eat, think, and speak while undergoing dialysis because of kidney failure. To Sharon, who is fiercely committed and fearless in creating and pursuing her dreams and makes "never having done it before" her reason for doing everything, including becoming, among many other things, a chiropractor, radio host, writer, business coach, traveler, and founder of Borrowed Wisdom. To Layla, a bright, creative, spiritual, and resourceful single woman who decided to risk making an investment in pursuit of a lifelong dream. To Julie, who decided to say goodbye to a season of relationships so that she could live in a more authentic way and then said hello to a new beginning. She became an author in her sixties and now regularly appears on podcasts, entertaining listeners with her "senior" stories. To Bonnie, who allowed herself the freedom to feel her feelings and open herself to exciting new work after being laid off and dealing with the sadness of her twin brother's stroke. To Dyana, who decided to embrace her curiosity and passion for reinvention and exploration that led to many diverse careers. To Mattie, who decided she was strong when she was suddenly widowed with five children and found a way to create a compelling future. To Aileen, who used deliberate thought work to make powerful decisions she never regretted. To M.J., who learned the value of managing her mind as a daily practice and as a means of redeciding what her heart condition meant. To Leah, Linda, Lisa, Ala, Brooke, and so many others who've shared their significant big and little decisions with me, I am grateful to you all.

To my editor Jessica Hatch, I appreciate your gentle nudges to make me dig deeper and for your keen skills at honing and polishing my words.

Finally, I am particularly indebted to Brooke Castillo, whose work has heavily influenced this book. Some ideas, models, and direct quotes are reprinted with permission from the author Brooke Castillo. Learn more at *www.brookecastillo.com*.

Reader Note:

Life Coaching is not a replacement for therapy. While the tools provided in this book can radically improve one's life, if you experience medically diagnosed depression, trauma, or PTSD, please seek the appropriate licensed mental health care providers to aid you.

**This book is dedicated to your future self,
the one who is depending on you to decide.**

TABLE OF CONTENTS

ACKNOWLEDGMENTS v
INTRODUCTION: Read This First 1

SECTION I: THE POWER OF YOUR DECISIONS 5

Chapter 1. Why Decisions Matter 7
Chapter 2. The Light Science of Decisions 17
Chapter 3. Decision Debt: What's the Cost of Indecision? 21
Chapter 4. Analysis Paralysis 33

SECTION II: YOUR PAST DECISIONS 41

Chapter 5. People Pleasing: Who am I Deciding for? . . 43
Chapter 6. Woulda, Coulda, Shoulda 53
Chapter 7. Arguing with the Past 57
Chapter 8. What Do You Make It Mean? 63

SECTION III: REDECIDING YOUR FUTURE 71

Chapter 9. Do You Want What You Have? 73
Chapter 10. Fear of Making the Wrong Decision 85
Chapter 11. Preventing Future Regret 99
Chapter 12. Mining the Gold of "Failed & Fabulous" Decisions 107

SECTION IV: PUTTING IT ALL TOGETHER 115

Chapter 13. The Secret Sauce of Intuition. 117

Chapter 14. As Soon As You Decide, Prepare to Be Challenged 121

Chapter 15. "Just Decide" Strategies. 125

Chapter 16. The Beauty of Never Getting It Done 133

~~~

KEEP THE JOURNEY GOING 141
~~~

INTRODUCTION: Read This First

There I was at sixty-five years of age, looking at my vision board for the year 2020. It needed a title and a theme. I asked myself, "What is the perfect word that will guide my intentions, thoughts, feelings, and actions for the next year?

"Is it 'clarity' or 'decisiveness'?"

Nothing like a little irony to start the year.

WHAT'S YOUR STORY?

Does indecision keep you stuck and stagnating in the same job or relationship? Does analysis paralysis cripple you when it comes to making health decisions? Does "all or none" thinking thwart you from going after your dream goals? Worse yet, have you simply stopped dreaming?

Do you wonder how your life would be different if you were confident, decisive, and aligned with creating the career, relationships, and health you desire?

What if there was an easy solution? Would you want to know?

What if I told you all you had to do was JUST DECIDE?

I imagine you chose this book because you already feel the negative effects of indecision. You are tired, stuck, and maybe even beating yourself up because you know you want something different but can't decide what or how to make it happen. Indecision drains you of your vital, creative mental energy and diminishes your trust in your own abilities. What's more, indecision costs you time and money.

The number one goal of this book is to help you trust yourself to make decisions. You will let go of the critical judgments of your past. You will redecide your future by choosing empowered thoughts and aligned feelings that fuel your actions for deliberately creating the life you want.

The book is divided into four sections: In Section 1, we'll explore the "Power of Decisions," why they matter, and how every aspect of your life is a result of a decision you've made deliberately or by default, even when conditions and circumstances happened that you *didn't* choose. Then, we will dive into the simplified neuroscience of understanding how and why your brain works. You'll become an expert at knowing when to disregard your primitive brain that keeps you in a state of fear and how to employ your analytical prefrontal cortex to become the CEO of your life. You'll discover the real cost of decision debt and how it impacts your time, emotions, and health. You'll recognize and deactivate the all too familiar dream crushers of analysis paralysis, confusion, and overwhelm. Finally, you'll practice your first strategy for making decisions by elevating your awareness of your thoughts.

Section II is all about your "Past Decisions." You'll discover why "people pleasing" is a lose-lose proposition and how to turn it around to win. You'll explore using simple language hacks to shape your life and take you from "should" and "have to," to the benefits of "want" and "get to," and on to the ultimate manifestation words, "I am." You'll be invited to edit, find meaning, and retell the story of your past so that it informs you of the future you want. You'll experiment by making small pivots in your behavior that ultimately lead to substantial long-term improvements in your health, finances, and relationships.

Section III will have you actively "Re-Deciding Your Future" by examining your present and deliberately deciding what's next in your life. You'll bust through the fears of making the wrong decision and learn what it takes to make the best decision. These exercises will teach you how to regret-proof your decisions while curating your exquisite, bespoke life.

Finally, Section IV has you "Putting it All Together." This section takes decision-making to the next level using your whole brain, not just your analytical reasoning. You'll learn to recognize, strengthen, and employ your superpowers of intuition, a skill Oprah Winfrey credits for her phenomenal successes. You'll learn to have your own back and use obstacles as the indicators of your next steps. You will be given the blueprint for following the steps to deciding the "big" decisions, the ones that may have multiple steps, time frames, or involve other people.

You will find Thought Gems 💎 at each chapter's end inviting you to JUST DECIDE a new thought that ultimately will create a new mindset.

This book is intentionally brief because it's not actually about goal setting. It's the precursor to goal setting. It's about deciding. It's about becoming a person who decides she wants to create a visible, vibrant, and vital life no matter her age.

The definition of "decision" actually has Latin roots and is a combination of two words:

de ("off") + *caedere* ("cut")

"Decide" means to cut off other options and commit to one.

How can you get the best results? Successful readers make the most progress by downloading the complimentary workbook and doing the thought work exercises, but a regular notebook of your choosing will also work. Just be sure to answer the questions posed in the book. The value of this is that you will gain enormous awareness to create the next steps of your deliberate, intentional life. But I caution you against two things. The first is to *never* use awareness as a weapon against yourself. Shaming, hating, criticizing, and beating yourself up for past decisions, behaviors, feelings, or thoughts will never bring you fulfillment, peace, or the attainment of the life you want. Bring kindness, curiosity, compassion, and the expectation that growth will be a little uncomfortable.

The second thing is that awareness without action will not create a new result. You must take action. Throughout this process, you will grow comfortable with "failed attempts" as the benchmark of your effort of pursuit. Instead of focusing on the failures, we will count the number of times you risk and try something as the measure of your success.

I'm excited to be on this journey of discovery with you. Set the intention right now to commit to learning and practicing the tools of *deciding* in order to up-level every decision of your life, relationships, career, and health. It's not about perfection; it's about truth, consistency, practice, and repetition. I promise you will grow more confident and capable by exercising your mind and by prioritizing the thoughts and behaviors that support you. You'll learn to have your own back and relinquish the need to please others at your expense. You will grow into true emotional adulthood through loving yourself and learning to keep your promises to yourself. You will elevate all of your relationships because of this newly found love affair with yourself.

I promise to lovingly remind you of the one life you have to live, the 86,400 seconds you have every day if you make it through the full twenty-four hours. You will grow to value your twenty-four hours as if they were a daily allowance of $24,000. You will decide how to spend that precious allowance to produce the greatest return on your investment.

Let's get to it because the next 86,400 seconds or $24,000 are yours to spend.

SECTION I

THE POWER OF YOUR DECISIONS

In this first section we'll explore the power of decisions, why they matter, and how every aspect of your life is a result of a decision you've made deliberately or by default, even when conditions and circumstances happened that you *didn't* choose. Next, we'll dive into the simplified neuroscience of understanding how and why your brain works. You'll discover the real cost of decision debt and how it impacts your time, emotions, and health. You'll recognize and deactivate the all too familiar dream crushers of analysis paralysis, confusion, and overwhelm. Finally, you'll practice your first strategy for making decisions.

CHAPTER 1 WHY DECISIONS MATTER

"Cumulatively small decisions, choices, actions, make a very big difference."

~ Jane Goodall ~

Making a decision is the most powerful thing you can do because decisions shape our destinies. Every day it's estimated we make around 25,000 to 30,000 micro-decisions, including whether to pick our noses or use a tissue. While it's true most of these are done unconsciously—make a cup of coffee, open the refrigerator, or scroll through texts—each of those decisions actually either supports you in reaching your goals or moves you further from them.

So often I hear my clients say, "I just don't know." This used to be my default as well. I'd rely on my partner or friend for the simple small choices: Hair up or down? Dress or pantsuit? These seemingly innocuous exchanges weren't wrong per se; they just made my own decision-making skills flabby. You see, the world wouldn't have come to an end if I wore my hair up or down, if I picked the blue dress over the striped pantsuit, but what did happen was I eroded my trust and confidence in myself to make decisions.

THE SMALLEST DECISIONS MAKE THE BIGGEST IMPACT

Why is making simple, seemingly unimportant decisions easily without collaboration so vital to developing the muscle of decision-making? Because doing so activates your trust and belief in yourself and fuels your confidence to take on bigger, more daring, and complex decisions. There is a time and place for consulting and collaboration with others, sure, but the better you get at trusting yourself, the more discerning you'll be when consulting with others on those decisions that require processing more complex information.

Imagine that little decisions are like little drops of water. One tiny drip from the roof onto the floor means nothing, no big deal, but now visualize one little drip every minute. That's sixty drips an hour or 1,440 drips a day multiplied by 365 days a year, adding up to a whopping 525,600 drops of water—and a whole lot of water damage!

On the flip side, let's say instead of allowing the water to drip on the floor, you capture it in vessels, store the water, and use it to water your vegetable garden. The result is you create a viable vegetable garden that feeds you.

The point is it's the cumulative effect of the decisions we make or that we avoid making that create the results we get. Indecision is actually a decision, but one that keeps us stuck. Ultimately we are the only ones responsible for our lives. Regardless of the relationships we share, we always have a choice. Every choice has a consequence, and we get to decide on purpose if we want to make that choice.

The "smallest" decisions are often the most powerful because they're happening all the time. Just think about it: One of the most important decisions occurs even before we get out of bed. The decision to hit snooze or get up when the alarm rings can radically change the trajectory of our lives because that very choice creates a pattern for our thoughts and behaviors about how we show up in the world.

We believe it is only the big choices that determine our futures, but the little, insidious decisions or indecisions ultimately determine our futures as well. Something as simple as looking at one's self in the mirror gives rise to a decision. What do you decide? Do you think you're too fat or old, too wrinkled or too gray? These unconscious decisions are created by our *thoughts*, which then create feelings of critical self-judgment that may ultimately lead to unhealthy or even destructive behaviors like compulsive bingeing or other eating disorders, obsessions with plastic surgery, or at the very least a poor self-image.

We think we are simply stating observations. We believe these are facts about ourselves, but in reality, these are thoughts. Opinions. A thought that is practiced repeatedly is hardwired into our brains and becomes part of our belief system (i.e., our BS), which then influences future decisions. This hardwiring of our brains is useful when the thoughts are empowering, but can have devastating consequences when they focus on what's perceived as an irrefutable limitation.

So the question is: Who's in charge of these thoughts? The answer is *we are*, but only if we elevate our awareness to the level of deliberate thoughts.

We have sixty to seventy thousand thoughts a day, and trust me, not all of them are worthy of Mother Teresa. It is our awareness and ability to question these thoughts and sort the empowering ones from the ones that belittle and bully us that allow us to strengthen our decision-making muscles. When your brain starts talking smack about and to you, it's a good idea to pause and ask, "Is that true? Do I want to believe it?"

(ONE OF) MY STORIES

I don't know why or when I started judging myself so harshly. I can't blame it on terrible parents or abuse; my parents were very loving and good. I do know I hungrily sought attention and validation. I was the middle child who seemed to do well enough on her own, so my parents trusted me to steer my own ship. My older sister, on the other hand, was more bent on carving her way and choosing her own thoughts. Often her choices were perceived as defiant and dangerous. She took risks that landed her in serious trouble, from the principal's office to the hospital. My parents took a full-court press to tame and regulate her behavior. My brain offered me this logic: Since my sister is getting all this attention for being really bad, maybe if I was really good or, better yet, really perfect, my parents would notice me more.

Had I known back then that those thoughts were optional, I could've decided to think other thoughts that might have saved me years of harm. The truth was, it was my thoughts about needing to be perfect, not my parents' attention or lack thereof, that made me anxious and driven, with frantic energy to perform, compete, achieve, excel, and parade around those accomplishments with a flag to get noticed. What I didn't realize at the time was the impact it caused. To soothe those anxious feelings of overwhelm and not-enoughness, I ate. Actually, I ate a lot. Of course, I did this secretly because overeating wasn't in my model of control. I also threw up in private because I was ashamed of being out of control. I cycled through a pattern of bingeing, purging, and hating myself. I routinely grabbed a handful of fat and lashed hateful criticisms at myself when I looked in the mirror. I never considered myself a self-destructive person, yet there I was, hurting myself. I was the perpetrator, all because I decided to believe thoughts without question.

Thankfully there was a loving part of me, who knew my worthiness was inherent and decided she'd had enough of hating and shaming and hurting. I was already in my late twenties, but I decided at that moment to stop throwing up and to stop saying hateful things to myself in the mirror. I decided I might not like what I saw in the mirror, but that I would say, "I LOVE YOU" out loud. I decided to love myself back to health and sanity. I decided to become aware of what I was eating and practice allowing my feelings by identifying them and noticing them. I actively practiced forgiveness of myself and the thought errors I had. I stopped blaming the circumstances and became compassionate. When I chose a diet of love, acceptance, and forgiveness instead of hate and blame, I learned to truly appreciate myself.

* * * *

If self-hate is the obvious esteem crusher, self-doubt is its trickier twin. Unexamined self-doubt can slowly and silently chip away at self-esteem and confidence. It's the type of doubt we assume is just the truth or an objective observation about ourselves. For example, "I'm not good at math" seems harmless enough unless it's the excuse you give yourself for never checking your bank balance and always being overdrawn or forgoing paying taxes because it's too complicated. But what if you were curious enough to question this "fact"? What if you chose a different thought, such as, "I can learn to manage my bank and get help from people who know more about finances"?

The point is we don't have to believe every thought that comes into our minds.

When your brain offers negative, bullying self-talk, remember to ask yourself, "Do I *choose* to believe this?" Learn to discern the thoughts that limit or hurt you from the ones that recognize your value and limitless potential. Believe thoughts that empower you.

WHAT ARE YOU DECIDING?

Are you aware that you are always making decisions in the four biggest areas of your life: health, relationships, career, and finances? Within those broad categories, there are many more subcategories. We haven't even tackled the spiritual or leisure areas of your life yet.

Health Decisions

- Eating/Food choices
- Drinking water and alcohol
- Sleeping
- Mindset
- Exercising

Relationship Decisions

- Choosing partners (e.g., gender, sexuality, monogamous, polyamorous)
- Marrying/Not marrying
- Children/No children (e.g., adoption, fostering, surrogacy)
- Expectations of others

Career Decisions

- Work
- School
- Business entrepreneur/Employee

Money Decisions

- ❍ Earning
- ❍ Spending
- ❍ Saving
- ❍ Investing

In any given category of your life, how often have you consciously or unconsciously outsourced this fundamental right to decide to others? Whether it's your cultural heritage, family doctrine, media-influenced messages, or even your circle of friends, have you asked yourself, "Am I deciding things based on my values?" Sometimes, especially as we grow older, we live with previously made decisions as if they are set in stone and no longer fall into the category of choice. I am going to challenge you to question this concept. Just because we've decided and done something in the past, do we have to repeat it? This includes everything we think we are supposed to do or have to do just because we have done it for so long, from simple decisions like re-evaluating the furniture you've had for the last twenty or more years to redeciding more significant things like your marriage agreements. This is not to say, "Let's stir up the pot," and look for problems where there aren't any. This is not a "Why fix something that's not broken?" strategy either. Neither of those thoughts could be further from the point. The purpose of this inquiry is to be aware, to decide in the present time, and to learn about wanting what you have and having what you want. This is not a midlife crisis. It's a midlife awakening.

The first strategy of decision-making is to elevate your awareness about the decisions you are already making.

THOUGHT GEM

JUST DECIDE Decisions small and large create your destiny. Elevate your awareness.

PAUSE AND REFLECT

What do you want in each of the categories below? What is important to you?

Health:

____

____

____

____

Relationships:

____

____

____

____

Career:

____

____

____

____

____

Money:

____

____

____

____

Personal Growth/Spirituality:

____

____

____

____

____

1. Write down *how* you spent the last twenty-four hours. Try and recall everything you did, including the time you slept, ate, worked, relaxed, called or talked to people, wrote, and checked social media.

2. What time did your day begin? When did it end? Did you hit snooze when the alarm went off?

   List everything you did. You will learn that behind the activities and things you did or didn't do were decisions you made deliberately or unconsciously.

The value here is in learning how much control you actually have for the choices you make based on where you put your focus and attention.

3. Ask yourself *why* you decided to do those things. Are they in alignment with what you think is most important?

4. Notice your reasons for your decisions. Do you like them?

5. Would you decide the same things again?

Remember, this is an exercise to stimulate curiosity, not judgment. Keeping this in mind, are these decisions in alignment with the desires you listed under the previous categories of health, relationships, career, money, and personal growth?

CHAPTER 2 THE LIGHT SCIENCE OF DECISIONS

"The human brain starts working the moment you are born and never stops until you stand up to speak in public."

~ George Jessel ~

You've just learned that making lots of decisions is the simplest way to build the practice of decision-making, especially if you take baby steps to strengthen your skills with low-impact decisions like what outfit to wear or which entree to order. These little daily drips add up to cumulative skills for the big ones, the epic decisions that could potentially change the course of your life. So before you start operating the heavy machinery (i.e., your prefrontal cortex, the part of your brain that functions as the executive and CEO), you might want to learn a little about your brain.

This chapter *will not* be exact science. Although my background as a speech and language pathologist working with people who've had traumatic brain injuries and strokes could cause me to go into the depths of our gray matter, this chapter will be the light science of the brain; that is, it will be a general framework for understanding and appreciating what your brain does on a daily basis. Seriously, we carry around the world's greatest, most complex computer, the only operating system that grows memory as it's used, and we give it so little appreciation.

Where do decisions occur and how are they made in the brain? In other words, what's going on between our thoughts and the actions we take to get our results?

Here's the simple explanation regarding the "where" anatomy of our brains: visualize a corporate-level organization with the

CEO at the top of the organization, a supervisor at the mid-level, and an entry-level employee at the bottom.

The lowest level of the brain is the oldest part, often known as the lizard brain or the reptilian brain. The lizard brain's sole function is to protect us and keep us alive. It's responsible for our basic, but vital, life functions such as heart rate, breathing, body temperature, and balance. It senses danger and responds to urges like ones for food, water, and sex. Think of this lowest part of your brain as an entry-level employee who responds to needs and keeps things running, but doesn't make any critical decisions.

Moving up to the midbrain or "supervisor level" is our emotional limbic system. This part of our brain enables us to have a wide variety of feelings and is the site of memory and motivation. Fear is one such feeling the limbic system creates, and it is the supervisor's job in the brain to always be on the lookout for anything that looks like, smells like, or sounds like a threat. The thing is the brain can't tell the difference between a real and an imagined threat, so whether you're being chased by a mugger or freaking out about the presentation you have to deliver in front of your colleagues, the brain activates the same stress response to either fight, flee, or freeze.

The top level, so to speak, is our brain's neocortex. This biological change to the human brain was an evolutionary game changer. The neocortex is the part of our brain where the prefrontal cortex (PFC) resides. The PFC is the chief executive officer (CEO) of your brain. Think of this part of your brain as Decision-Making Central. It's the big boss that plans, organizes, integrates, and processes all of your sensory information and memory and then executes action based on all that data.

Of course, these distinct brain structures do not operate independently. Your brain lights up like a pinball machine when making decisions. It goes to the past, remembers sensory information, then projects to the unknown future, and brings with it either fear or pleasurable memories associated with previous similar decisions, and it does this at lightning speed.

The purpose of this explanation is simply to give you a working understanding of how your brain functions; how to know when your lizard brain is trying to protect you or when your emotional brain is having a tantrum; and how to love and integrate all those parts while allowing your CEO brain, your prefrontal cortex, to make executive decisions and be in charge of the grown-up you.

Your lizard brain will screech when you want to contemplate doing something "dangerous" or "life-threatening," like speaking to a person you don't know but want to meet; it will send out red alerts when you're launching a new business, signaling you to go back to the safety of the cave. Your midbrain will remind you of all your past failures as a means to keep you safe from exploring new territories. It will amplify your doubts and keep you in analysis paralysis when you contemplate making a move to a new city, leaving an old job, or beginning or ending a relationship. With the best intentions, your lower brain will cause you to abandon your dreams in favor of safety rather than risk dying in pursuit of evolving. This can cause you to feel stuck because you have one foot on the gas pedal of your dreams and the other foot on the fear and doubt brake. No wonder we burn rubber, get exhausted, and end up going nowhere.

Now that you have the owner's manual to your brain, you're prepared to forge ahead and undertake some reflective exercises. In the following chapters, you will increasingly gain awareness of your brain's default protective mechanism that may have you either going unconscious or catastrophizing the worst-case scenario. Remember, your brain only wants three things: to keep you alive and out of danger, to seek pleasure, and to conserve energy. From this heightened state of awareness, you can have compassion and curiosity—not to let yourself off the hook or to give yourself a "pass" for inaction, but to truly understand why you did or didn't take action based on how you felt, which of course was driven by the thoughts you were thinking.

THOUGHT GEM

JUST DECIDE to make decisions using your high-level prefrontal cortex–that is the CEO of your brain.

CHAPTER 3 DECISION DEBT: WHAT'S THE COST OF INDECISION?

"More is lost by indecision than wrong decisions. Indecision is the thief of opportunity. It will steal you blind."

~ Marcus Tullius Cicero ~

Have you ever said, "I just can't make another decision!" Decision fatigue is real. I remember saying that to the poor waiter at a restaurant. We'd just come from a three-hour meeting with an estate planning attorney where my husband and I decided upon everything we wanted to happen in the event that we died and left our only minor daughter an orphan. I was exhausted and famished and just wanted a salad.

When the server innocently asked, "Do you want the salad chopped or full leaf? Dressing on the salad or on the side? Croutons, no croutons? Cheese, no cheese? Protein, no protein?" what I really wanted to say was, "Skip the salad! Bring me a bowl of ice cream!"

The truth was it wasn't the questions; I was just out of decision gas and too fatigued from the early heftier decisions I'd just made for the last several hours.

Decision fatigue is our brain's stopgap measure to avoid overheating and blowing a circuit. It lets us default into immediate relief in order to avoid pain. It goes for quick and easy immediate gratification. Decisions made while in a state of decision fatigue are rarely if ever the ones that propel you to your highest self. These decisions are not for your ultimate growth. They may pacify and placate you for the moment, but the consequences of these types of decisions ultimately lead to poor self-esteem, potential addiction, and deeply wired neural networks that go for immediate gratification instead of long-term fulfillment and satisfaction.

THE COST OF INDECISION

Decision debt is a lot like financial debt. If you think of decisions as brain energy you spend, then you can think of this brain energy as actual currency. When you have the money to spend on an item you desire, you pay for it, and that's that. When you don't, you borrow money, put it on your credit card, and delay the time at which it will need to be paid back. The thing is, whatever you've delayed or put on credit actually costs more because of interest, so yes, you get it right away, but typically by the time it's paid off, the thrill of having the thing has vanished and the dread of paying for your past weighs you down.

Decision debt is about big things: careers, relationships, and health. These are the pivotal forks in the road. Pausing to be reflective and not in a hurry, pausing to anticipate potential outcomes, and pausing to check in with your future self are excellent uses of your prefrontal cortex. Remember from Chapter 2 that this is the CEO part of the brain that allows you to plan, anticipate, and execute. Where it gets dicey is staying at the fork in the road and setting up camp. This indecision or resistance to following our desire to expand is what drains us, keeps us feeling stuck and not going anywhere except deeper into a state of misbelief about our potential, our ability to create, and our ability to have the life we know at our core is our calling.

You can recognize decision debt by these hallmark words: "I don't know. I'm not ready to make a decision." It could be as innocuous as the dresses you've tried on but need validation from others before you can purchase or the phrase "I can't start my business because I don't know how."

Decision debt usually stems from the fear of making the right decision or, worse yet, making the wrong decision. Our brains can catastrophize in great detail all the things that could go wrong. It's funny how when I suggest people practice visualization to create intended, deliberate, and desired goals, they often say, "I can't visualize," yet when I ask them to think about the move across the country they're contemplating, they can picture in great detail their mom's sad face and lament: "You can't leave me." They viscerally feel the knot in their stomach over deciding whether to pack or toss the box of scribbles their three-year-old child drew twenty-five years ago. They see themselves drinking alone with their cat as they eat popcorn for dinner. In fact, these same people who don't know how to visualize can provide IMAX details of everything they will see, hear, feel, smell, and taste as they think about the scary decision that intrigues and excites them yet simultaneously terrifies them.

The problem with this feature film is that it chronicles *imagined* risks, not real ones. Meanwhile, decision debt is costly in three areas: it drains our time, our physical wellness, and our emotional wellbeing.

***Not* deciding is actually deciding.**

TIME DEBT

Have you ever researched the best flight reservation but couldn't pull the decision trigger quickly enough so the last seat got booked and you lost out? What about repeatedly researching the best doctor, school, neighborhood, therapist, the cheapest gas, the best restaurant, and *not* making a decision? We know indecision wastes precious time. Sure, it makes you look busy (as if there were medals for busyness), but it ultimately slows your momentum and keeps you exactly where you were, if not further behind.

Time is the only commodity we all share regardless of how rich or poor we are, our cultural heritage, our religion, or our gender. There is no time guarantee for anyone, though in the bigger sense, the older we get, it's pretty safe to say we can expect less time ahead. I understand the reality of time as I write this book as a sixty-six-year-old woman; there is certainly less life ahead of me than there is behind me.

That said, decision debt gets more costly with every incomplete decision. The failure to decide to pursue a career that's always called to you or to get your health back on track drains your energy. That's not to say every decision should be a yes. The full Amazon shopping cart cultivated by the urge to assuage your feelings instead of calling your friend with whom you've had a fight may be best left unbought. Perhaps the better question here is, "What's the best decision I can make with the limited time I have on earth?"

Have you ever said, "I have time to kill," or worse, "I need to kill some time"? We take these expressions lightly, as if they have no significance, but the reality is they do. Time is not a renewable resource. Killing time dismisses it as insignificant and not worthy of reverence. You don't have to do something "epic" like cure cancer in the twenty minutes you have to wait for your doctor's appointment, but *kill* time? What if you considered the twenty-minute wait a golden opportunity to drop into a state of conscious breathing and mindfulness? Even a few minutes of mindfulness practice can help relieve stress, lower blood pressure, reduce chronic pain, and alleviate gastrointestinal difficulties. It also helps with reducing worry and anxiety.

PHYSICAL WELLNESS DEBT

Decision debt hurts us physically. Did you know that 80 percent of all medical doctor's visits are related to stress? We all know "stress is a killer," but this vague, undetermined myriad of symptoms, from headaches and gastric problems to muscle aches, fatigue, sleeplessness, weight gain, overdrinking, high blood pressure, and so on has its roots in decision debt.

What shows up as a physical result is the body's way of coping with internal conflict. We have all spent a sleepless night arguing the pros and cons of leaving a relationship, having a difficult conversation, deciding to quit or start a job, or rehashing a medical report. We pop pills to manage the headaches and stomachaches that accompany the decisions that lie ahead; however, prolonging indecision exacerbates our condition.

Decision debt drains us of vital energy and therefore of our physical wellness. We feel sluggish when we carry the weight of indecision. Our energy stagnates. Our physical vibration is lower and denser.

EMOTIONAL WELLNESS DEBT

How is procrastination linked to emotional debt? Procrastination is simply not doing the thing you've decided to do. It's like being on hold endlessly while tying up the phone line. It drains your battery. The more you forgo the decision to initiate action toward the thing you decided to do, the more you deplete your desire, stamina, and resourcefulness. It creates a domino effect that makes us want to hide from ourselves and everyone else.

Someone might ask, "How's that book you're working on?"

"Uh, you mean the one I've decided to not work on by simply not deciding to get to work on it?"

This pile of incomplete decisions drains you of mental energy because the brain likes completion. It likes to have answers to questions. It goes on high alert, asking, "What about this? Are you going to take the job? Are you going to sign up for that class you wanted? When are you planning that trip? Are you going to talk to your mother about why you don't answer her texts at five in the morning?" This barrage of unanswered questions puts our brains on high alert and causes anxiety.

Yep, that's right; it just might be that if you experience anxiety on the regular, you should look at the list of unfinished projects, unanswered emails, abandoned goals, and clutter in your closet, inbox, drawers, and garage. All of this unfinished business is the evidence of decisions left to languish because of discomfort, fear, self-doubt, and indecision.

Decision debt hurts us emotionally because it tends to reinforce the self-concept that we're not capable. We may hold on to a false concept of ourselves as "cautious" as a means of protection, but over time decision debt weakens our willingness to come out of the cave and expand ourselves. We let our self-esteem atrophy and limit our lives by delaying and not deciding. We think we are protecting ourselves, but in reality, we are thwarting our growth and minimizing ourselves.

How do I know this? Because I see this with so many of my clients who report this problem. I also intimately know about indecision. For all the many things I've done and accomplished in my life, my decision debt has cost me physically and emotionally, and it has cost me the most important resource of all—time. I was an action taker who certainly looked busy, but much like a truck stuck in a mud puddle, the harder I pushed on the gas of busyness, the deeper I dug my wheels into the mud. I didn't appreciate my time or respect it. I set no healthy boundaries on my time, which led to overwork and exhaustion.

Before I learned to manage my mind and my thoughts, I was indecisive and agonized about spending money. Growing up with a mindset that had me believe that money was a finite resource that would be lost once I spent it prevented me from resourceful thinking, including leveraging money to create things that would ultimately result in more abundance. Most of all, indecision created anxiety. I didn't call it that, I never felt like I suffered from anxiety, but I felt restless and uncomfortable, so I soothed myself with eating to guard myself from that uncomfortable feeling. This "soothing activity" created its own problem of being overweight, which caused me to put all of my focus on my weight and what I was eating instead of on what was eating *me,* which was the fact that I wasn't doing what I said I wanted to do. Learning to manage my mind put me back in control and moving forward.

"WHEN LIFE HAPPENS" DECISIONS

You may have climbed on board the "decision debt is bad" bandwagon. You may even be out in front, banging your drum about it. But what about the decisions we don't want to have to make? The ones about sad, bad, or otherwise scary parts of life?

The truth is unforeseen circumstances happen. You might be the type of person who has a healthy diet, who exercises, who meditates and feels gratitude, but all the same, things do happen. You or a loved one might get a sudden diagnosis of cancer, or a freak accident may occur in which a drunk driver crashes into your house while you're sleeping in your bed. Things do happen. People die. These are the events of our lives over which we sometimes have no control. These events may change the course of your life, but with the exception of severe brain damage that literally destroys your ability to make choices, you will always retain your ability to respond to the new circumstances by deciding what you will make them mean.

This is by no means a Pollyanna moment in which I'll say everything happens for a reason; whether that is true is for you to decide. Yet there are some who experience what many would describe as catastrophic events (e.g., a stroke, a tumor, a car accident) that have had massive, life-altering effects, and they view these events as life-enhancing. I can't tell you how many stories my clients who've suffered strokes and brain injuries have shared in which they talk about the great gifts they've gotten as a result of those events, such as the alcoholic who became sober as a result of his stroke and is so grateful to have been liberated from the paralyzing and debilitating condition of alcoholism. Having worked with thousands of people who have experienced severe health challenges, I am always reminded that it is our thoughts, not our circumstances, that create our outcomes. My clients often discover how badass they actually are. They recognize their own resilience and sometimes report the deep love they felt toward and from others. They often speak about a newfound faith that came to them unexpectedly. I'm not saying this happens for everyone, but this known fact of *post-traumatic growth* comes from one's thoughts. The circumstance didn't change, but the mindset and thoughts did. Read Leslie's story to see how her mindset, not her circumstances, changed.

LESLIE'S STORY

The doctor said, "You have stage 4 uterine cancer."

I felt a gut punch that brought me to tears, but honestly, almost immediately, my thought was, "I cheated death once; cancer is not going to kill me."

I barely let the doctor finish speaking when he said, "I believe surgery, chemo, and radiation will be your best opportunity to heal, but first we need to do some preliminary things."

"I've already done those things. Can we schedule the surgery in the next few days? I want the cancer removed."

Deciding on surgery, chemo, and radiation seemed relatively minor compared with my decision to maintain a positive attitude while going through these processes. While I believed that attitude was as important as medicine in the healing process, I also recognized I had some thoughts to clean up. FIrst, I chose not to go down the "why me" path. Why not me? How was I different from any other person diagnosed with cancer? I wasn't any better or worse of a person. Why not me? Having witnessed my mother, a couple of aunts, cousins, and my two best friends live and even thrive during their medical ordeals with heart disease, MS, COPD, and cancer, I knew that I came from "good stock."

Then, I decided to remove any negative people from my inner circle. I chose to be surrounded only by positivity. I decided that laughter would help me heal, so I started watching silly comedies, funny movies, and reading funny stories. I read uplifting stories of people not only about cancer survival but also about survival in general. I knew my recovery was as much up to me as my practitioners, so during both radiation and chemo, I visualized tiny little samurai soldiers traveling through my body, obliterating any cancer cells. I followed my nurse practitioner's advice. She told me, "No matter how tired you feel"—and this was a tiredness that was beyond anything I could imagine—"get up every morning and get dressed." I decided that getting dressed and taking a nap in the living room was a mark of success and accomplishment. I decided to hack my language and choose my words carefully, realizing I was not "sick"; rather, I was "healing"!

While I'd never been a person who meditated, through the guidance of my sister, Tsgoyna (my most incredible advocate on my path to healing), I learned a few techniques of meditation and positive imagery. "Seeing" myself healing was very empowering. Listening to meditative instrumental music from around the world comforted and relaxed me.

Asking for help was my next mindset shift. Having a somewhat controlling personality, I had to make a conscious decision to allow myself to not only accept help from those around me but to actually ask for help. While it was challenging, I knew it was critical since I really couldn't do it all by myself. I chose to do whatever I could do and not let being unable to walk or have much stamina keep me from doing things I knew would bring me joy. I embraced using a wheelchair to go to museums, art galleries, or on nature walks. Nothing was going to stop me from enjoying life. I wasn't waiting until I felt better to enjoy it. I decided to practice enjoying life in advance of feeling better. I also visualized my future self, when I would no longer need assistance in doing these things.

Patience was never my strong suit, so it was interesting that I had to become a patient in order to learn patience. Gratitude was another conscious decision. I thanked God daily for the support system I had from my husband, my family, and my boss. I was struck by the many people I met at chemo who did not have the same kind of support. I had it easy. I concentrated on wanting and appreciating what I had.

What did I make getting a cancer diagnosis mean? That it would motivate, not hinder, either my attitude or my wellness. While I knew nothing was guaranteed, I somehow knew I would overcome my illness.

I had cheated death at twenty-one when I was run over by a motorcycle and lost my spleen and a kidney. I knew I had it in me to cheat death again! Ten years later, while in remission, I am reaping the benefits of my decisions.

* * * *

Leslie made many powerful decisions, and each one began with a thought. She recognized her thoughts were the source of all her power. Healing and recovery require deliberate thoughts. Will some people die regardless of how deliberate and intentional their thoughts are? Yes. But it's also possible to arrive at peace and acceptance about life's inevitable ending if you are managing your mind.

THOUGHT GEM

Indecision is a thief. JUST DECIDE to make any small decision to move you forward. You can course correct along the way.

PAUSE AND REFLECT

Although this chapter has been all about decision debt, the truth is, regardless of your debt, you've also made many decisions in your life. The value of these exercises is to cultivate, then point the light on the decisions you've made. Be bold and compassionate with yourself as you dive into this next exercise. *Decide in advance to love yourself through this exercise even if the decisions you made did not turn out how you wanted.*

REMINDER

Writing your answers down instead of just thinking about them enables you to see them with new insight.

Your Six Most Important Decisions

Pick the six most important decisions you've ever made regardless of how old you were when you made them. These might be decisions you made to either *do* or *stop doing* things. Plan to have an objective point of view as you let the memory reel roll. That means that you should be the observer who is describing what you decided.

If you haven't already downloaded the free *digital workbook,* do it now by using this link to make the most out of your experience with this book!

NOTE

You can always use a notebook of your choosing, but the workbook makes it easier by allowing you to see the questions/prompts.

The Six Most Important Decisions I've Made

1. ______________________________

2. ______________________________

3. ______________________________

4. ______________________________

5. ______________________________

6. ______________________________

Here are some examples of my most important decisions:

1. Go to graduate school
2. Quit job and become an aerobic instructor in Italy
3. Get married
4. Have a child
5. Write my first book
6. Change careers when I was turned sixty

Now for each of these decisions, answer the two questions below. We will explore other questions about these pivotal decisions in future chapters.

1. How did making this one decision change the course of your life?

____

____

2. How did making this decision influence your thoughts about yourself?

____

____

Set your timer for fifteen minutes and free-write your answers without stopping until the timer goes off. If you get stuck and nothing seems to flow from your pen or pencil, just keep writing the question prompts.

Make sure to do this for all six of your most important decisions. It is often in the hindsight of being able to connect the dots that we see the value of what looked like our missteps, misfortune, or misguided direction. Alternatively, we can see the value of what worked and went well; it may give us an opportunity to acknowledge ourselves and feel proud. "Failed" decisions are often the fertilizer of future successes. Read more about failure in Chapter 12, "Mining the Gold of Failed Decisions."

CHAPTER 4 ANALYSIS PARALYSIS

"I'm indecisive because I see eight sides to everything."

~ Anonymous ~

Decisions Fall into Two Categories:
Convicted or Conflicted

If you're reading this chapter, it's likely you relate to the concept of overthinking, overanalyzing, and overdoing everything except for over-delivering results. Chances are you are super smart with the brain capacity to see the nuance of every decision with 360-degree vision. You can create a robust pros and cons list and present stellar, courtroom-worthy defenses for both sides. You may actually even be an attorney. In my anecdotal experience, lawyers often suffer from this particular brain trick of analysis paralysis. For the brainiac, this is an acceptable version of indecision based on the supremely acceptable qualities of thoughtfulness, thoroughness, and measured deliberateness, but the truth is it's just a buffed-up version of fear-based indecision.

When you're truly "on to your brain's tricks," you can decide if those are the thoughts you want to continue to have or if other thoughts could lead you to feeling more certainty. Think back to a time where certainty empowered you to take actions that enabled you to create the outcome you desired.

I remember going to the pharmacy once with a throbbing headache. I do not routinely take medicine, not even something as common as aspirin, so when I scanned the shelves of literally hundreds of products and read each label, my headache worsened. Did I need aspirin, acetaminophen, or an NSAID? How many milligrams? Then I had to consider the precautions—don't even get me started on having to decide whether I wanted the meds that could possibly cause liver failure or lip smacking and delirium. Yeah, you guessed it: I walked out with nothing, but maybe that was the best decision after all.

Sometimes indecision is like a white flag of surrender, allowing you to decide in advance that you will be OK with whatever the outcome is. It's the *Que sera sera* version. As long as you like your reasons for not deciding and simply allowing whatever will be to be, that's good enough.

It only gets tricky if you are tormented by your indecision. Typically this happens with the bigger, weightier decisions like:

1) Do I marry the guy who's cheated on me three times since we've been living together, but who is my soulmate in every other way?

2) Do I move across the country and leave a relationship, friends, and family behind because I've always dreamed of this travel opportunity and work experience?

3) Do I have the surgery because the doctors say it's my best chance to beat cancer, even if it doesn't feel right to me?

Paralysis by overanalysis can simply stop us in our tracks. If your life has that déjà vu, "it's Groundhog Day all over again" feeling, you might want to widen your lens and see if this is an area of growth to consider.

THE IMPOSTER TWINS THAT KEEP YOU STUCK: CONFUSION AND OVERWHELM

How often do you find yourself saying, "I don't know what to do? I don't know how to do it," or, "There's just too much to do, and I don't have time. I can't get this all done." All too frequently we believe that confusion and overwhelm are irrefutable facts. We believe we're simply making an observation of truth when we say we are confused or overwhelmed. The thing is when we slip into this state of (mis)belief, we in fact create the result of being stuck, remaining confused, and wasting time. We actually block ourselves from finding the answers and taking action. Just for fun, imagine someone offers you $1 million to get done the very thing you say you don't know how to do and can't find the time to do. Do you think you'd have the same response? Would you be willing to at least begin? Would you be willing to Google, search on YouTube, ask everyone you know, try something, fail, and see what else you could do? My guess is your answer would be *yes*! You would find a way and *make* time a priority for achieving the thing.

This is why I call confusion and overwhelm the twin imposters. They masquerade around as large, looming, and very important feelings, but these indulgent emotions do not serve you when it comes to fulfilling your growth and expansion. Confusion and overwhelm prevent you from looking at the real feelings of fear you're likely experiencing. It is easier and more socially acceptable to be confused and overwhelmed than to deal with your deepest fears that you'll fail or be rejected. Just think back to how many conversations about your confusion and overwhelm you've had with your bestie, partner, boss, and anyone else who'll listen. The only way through overwhelm and confusion is... drumroll, please... to follow the alphabet.

Awareness Breath Curiosity Decide Experiment/Evaulate

How could using the alphabet help? Let's take a real-life example, but please know this is a simplified version for the purpose of illustration. Picture this: You've got six reports to write. Your boss keeps calling to add one more thing to your to-do list. Your computer is in spinny mode, and you know staying late at the office will put you in heavy traffic. You think, "This is impossible. I have too much to do and not enough time." You feel overwhelmed. As a result of feeling overwhelmed, you ruminate about all the things that aren't working. You gather evidence to support why you can't get your work done and share it with anyone who'll listen. You don't consider any alternatives for managing the work or dealing with the computer. You don't focus on one thing, but instead try multitasking, which results in more errors. Your stress escalates. The result you create is even less time to accomplish your tasks. You think the problem is the workload, but really the thought, "It's impossible. I don't have enough time" is what prevents you from resourcefully thinking, prioritizing tasks, and efficiently utilizing the time you have to complete anything.

So how can the alphabet help?

First become **aware** of the thought you are telling yourself. Slow your **breath** for just a couple of minutes to deactivate the stress response that has all the blood leaving your prefrontal cortex and reasoning abilities to flood your limbs with hormones to fight, flee, or freeze. Get **curious** about what other thoughts you might consider besides "It's impossible." **Decide** what you want to think and feel to make a tiny move forward. **Experiment** by taking one small action step toward your outcome and **evaluate** if that works or if a new action is needed.

Are there ever situations where overwhelm and confusion are justified and not only understandable? Of course, and yet you can still move beyond that frozen, stuck space. Listen to Mattie's story to learn how she faced her most profound decision while in a state of overwhelm, confusion, and despair.

MATTIE'S STORY

Maybe it was the soft bread or the crunchy cucumbers combined with the tangy mayonnaise... Whatever it was, I was overwhelmed and couldn't decide how and when to move on with my life. You see, my husband of twenty-four years had just died. I was the sole parent to our five children ages fifteen and under.

I know there really isn't a tangible connection between cucumber sandwiches and decision-making, but the most profound decision I ever made happened while I was eating that cucumber sandwich.

You see, as I chewed that sandwich, trying to process all the tastes and textures, I also tried to form a cohesive plan about everything I needed to do and how I would do it. The sandwich felt like glue in my mouth. My mind was stuck and mired in mud, spinning out the same thoughts over and over, getting nowhere.

I'd been raised in a fundamentalist religion and married my sweetheart. Together he and I built a beautiful home and started raising a family. We did all the things we were supposed to do. We were busy with kids, family, and church activities, and this amazing life was rolling out before us.

Maybe because we were so busy with the children and life, and certainly because there was such a stigma around mental health, I didn't realize it when the mental health challenges began to overtake my husband's heart, mind, and soul. I'm not sure he realized it either, as denial and minimization can be such strong coping mechanisms. Small decisions were made day after day to ignore reality, and in the end, we all lost.

You see, sometimes it's not the big decisions that are life-changing. Sometimes it's those very, very small decisions that change your path in unimaginable ways.

That day in the kitchen, when the full brunt of my husband's death settled down upon me, I made the decision to look reality in the face and not minimize or deny it, but to gather my strength and finish that one bite of sandwich that was in my mouth. I knew every other decision moving forward would revolve around this next pivotal choice. Would I cave into despair and depression, or would I press forward with positivity, determination, and strength? It really was simple, yet so very hard.

I chose to move forward, and my cucumber sandwich was my mountain. I decided to set the timer on the microwave for fifteen seconds because I knew I could make it through the next fifteen seconds. I stood by the stove eating my sandwich, fifteen seconds at a time. I decided that if I could make it through the first fifteen seconds, I could make it through the next fifteen seconds, and when the timer went off, I swallowed and repeated the cycle until my sandwich was gone.

One bite at a time, I made it through. Each bite was a conscious choice. Did my sandwich taste any better once I made that initial decision? No. In fact, the rest of the sandwich tasted like glue and cardboard. But that day, I decided I was strong, and I was going to be OK, and that was my choice.

* * * *

Mattie made a powerful decision at that moment. From a place of utter despair and not knowing, she decided she *was* strong. Not that she was going to be strong, but that she already was. She decided that *if* she was strong, she and her family would be OK. This didn't mean that Mattie's singular decision turned the ensuing minutes, days, and years into a rainbow, sugar-coated Hallmark movie, but she cut off any decision to think that she was incapable. Did she ask for help? Did she seek outside resources? Did she still grieve? Yes to all of that, but her thought, "*I AM STRONG*," created feelings of determination that led to the thousands of action steps that followed. All of those actions turned out to be the "hows" of what was originally causing her mind to be mired in mud and stuck with the thoughts, "I don't know what to do or how to do it."

I am not suggesting Mattie's experience is the gold standard for grieving or that everyone can make that immediate leap under those conditions, but this dramatic example shows us that, even though the circumstance didn't change at all, her thought was the fulcrum point that shifted everything.

PAUSE AND REFLECT

Choose a situation or circumstance you are currently thinking about in which you are desiring to make a decision but feel confused or overwhelmed. Ask yourself, "Is there anything else I might be feeling (fear, shame, embarrassment) below the surface of being confused and overwhelmed?"

Give yourself the chance to write your feelings here. Seeing your own words will bring clarity.

1. What else are you feeling besides confused and overwhelmed that is keeping you stuck?

____

____

____

____

2. What do you think you currently don't know that you will need to learn?

____

____

____

____

3. What would you do if you weren't confused?

____

____

____

4. List everything you "need" to do that is causing you to feel overwhelmed. Keep asking, "What else?"

____

____

____

____

5. Now, look at your "overwhelm" list. Knowing that you can't do everything at once, can you see a way to prioritize, delegate, or eliminate any items or extend the time frame in which everything needs to be done?

____

____

____

____

6. Look at your newly reordered list and ask, "What would I need to believe and feel in order to accomplish each individual task? What might I feel (i.e., what emotion would I have) if I made a decision? How does *not* making a decision impact me?"

____

____

____

____

SECTION II

YOUR PAST DECISIONS

In these next several chapters we'll explore the flip side of people-pleasing, how simple language hacks can positively shape decisions, and how rewriting the past and defining the meaning of circumstances leads to powerful shifts that set the groundwork for the future.

CHAPTER 5 PEOPLE PLEASING: WHO AM I DECIDING FOR?

"I can't tell you the key to success, but the key to failure is trying to please everyone."

~ Ed Sheeran ~

My client called to tell me she wanted to move to Seattle, but struggled with her decision because her friend didn't want her to leave.

Her friend begged, "Stay! I need you here. Plus, why do you want to go somewhere you don't have a job or place to live or me! Don't go!"

Another client, a doctor, considered a job opportunity but didn't want her husband to feel pressured to move, so she didn't share her excitement or enthusiasm for what she believed would be a great professional experience.

Have you ever made a decision to make someone else happy? Obviously we don't always make decisions in a vacuum. We reason that our decisions are based on others, such as when a parent or child needs us. We think it would be irresponsible to uproot a child and move them to a new location and school. We worry about our kids' responses to divorce or separation and what that would mean to the children who have no vote or control over the situation. You may be nervous to leave your job because the boss took a chance on you and gave you a great opportunity when no one else did, but now you have other aspirations and an urge to move on. Even health decisions can be made on the basis that we think they will please and satisfy someone else.

If we believe that one will win and one will lose by making a decision, we have already lost. Is it unrealistic to think that everyone will like a decision just because we've decided something? No, but the truth is we can't manage other people's feelings or thoughts. We can only manage our own. In short, by trying to please everyone, we end up pleasing no one, and the one who suffers most is ourselves. Failing to be our authentic self and follow our internal guidance and wisdom is the most common regret spoken about by people on their deathbeds. (See Chapter 11, "Preventing Future Regret").

My client Kendra spoke about how she could never say no to someone who asked her to do something or go somewhere. She told me a friend asked her to come to a party and she said yes, but then another person asked her to go out that same night with the girls. She didn't want to disappoint this other person, so she said yes to that too. Then a family member told her about a get-together that same night, and once again she said she'd be there. In the end she went to all three events, but was late to each of them and left early from all of them. I asked her how she felt about it, and she said, "Everyone was pissed at me, and I was exhausted. I didn't have any fun at all."

For Kendra it wasn't so much the fear of missing out as it was the fear of disappointing people, which of course in the end actually happened. Kendra now could see that her thought, "I don't want to disappoint people," had caused her to feel anxious and desperate to please everyone, resulting in her overpromising and under-delivering, which led her to the very outcome of disappointing everyone, including herself.

What may underlie the behavior of people-pleasing is a desire to avoid conflict and or gain love, approval, and validation from others. So often people pleasers simply think they're being nice, and what's wrong with being nice? Nothing, as long as being nice is not a means to an end, as long as it is not done in order to gain a sense of self-worth or validation, nor to suppress one's true feelings in order to avoid conflict. No one ultimately benefits from people-pleasing because there is always an unspoken sense of obligation to which the people pleaser feels entitled.

It's impossible to live an authentic life and feel as if you are in control if you are constantly choosing to live someone else's desires.

The following stories illustrate the flip side of people-pleasing; that is, the power of pleasing oneself and how that is the greatest expression of authenticity.

WHEN YOUR "YES" IS LOUDER THAN EVERYONE ELSE'S "NO!"

Have you ever had the experience where you unequivocally knew what was best? You felt certainty despite all the naysayers. No amount of dissenting opinions could have prevented you from doing what you knew was a "Hell yeah!" for yourself.

MY "HELL YEAH!" STORY

I made the decision to leave my career as a speech pathologist in my mid-twenties only two years after I'd earned my master's degree, begun a clinical practicum year, and completed my first year as a practitioner treating stroke survivors and those with brain injuries. I'd pursued my education for six years and practiced for two years, and suddenly I announced that I wanted to "develop my physical side." Back then I was unhappy with my circumstances. I felt a bit like a fraud. In fact, being so young and working with people in their fifties, sixties, and seventies, I felt more like a friendly visitor than a professional that had something valuable to offer. I was frustrated by the slowness of recovery and the long days of driving and inactivity. My body longed to move fast, and working in this field was the exact opposite of everything I yearned for. Yes, I thought that if I changed my circumstances, I would be happier. So I made decisions.

I quit my job, sold my car, gave up my apartment, and went on a trip to Mexico to a Club Med thinking I'd get a job as an exercise trainer. This was in the seventies, before cell phones and the internet. I had zero evidence that any of that could happen, but my thought was, "Why not now?" I was in my late twenties, unmarried, without a child, and I had no one to "answer to" but myself. I didn't rely on my parents for support; in fact, I lived in California and they lived in Florida, so we only saw each other a couple of times a year.

Everyone questioned me. "Why would you give up your education, career, and a viable means of support to go off to some unknown location and hope something will work out?"

Was I really choosing a different circumstance, or was I choosing to follow an impulse that was so strong, clear, and aligned even though there was no certainty, no guarantee, and no plan B in case it failed?

I reasoned I could always come back and start again, get another job, and make decisions from there if things didn't work out. The desire to take the risk was so much more compelling than the known path I was traveling. In the end, I actually did work for Club Med for a while. I traveled for two months in Mexico, met some amazing people, and had extraordinary experiences. I also got hepatitis, eventually returned home, and determined my next career move. The value of heeding my strong internal "Hell yeah!" far outweighed the cost of trying to please others.

* * * *

While my "Hell Yeah!" moment focuses on a decision I made for myself in early adulthood, Julie's story shows us how, in a later season of her life, she reassessed her deepest values and desires against the context of the long-standing friendships she had shared for many years.

JULIE'S STORY

Pop! The champagne cork flew into the universe, burying itself in the deep, dark depths of the Pacific Ocean. The super yacht rocked from side to side, blending caviar and fresh lobsters in my digestive system.

"Julie! Top up?" my host asked.

I felt nauseous but still offered my glass. I stopped counting the drinks I'd had. I swallowed what felt like poison, believing I was expected to. I engaged in superficial banter and celebrity gossip while drowning in a fog of apathy. This was meant to be fun. These people were my friends.

I'd circulated in this "hood" for years. We met up regularly and could even name each other's dogs and pet fish. Once docked, my husband and I scrambled down the exit ramp.

"Did you have fun?" inquired the host.

"Yes! Wonderful! Thank you!"

With the ocean in our rearview mirror, I turned to my husband, looked him straight in the eye, and said…

"Never again!"

"Never again? Why never again?"

What had changed so dramatically?

In deep reflection I realized it was me; I was the one who had changed.

I loved these friends in our season of commonality. We had formed friendships in our children's school halls and as enthusiastic sideline spectators on the sporting field.

But now, there was no school, and the thin thread of shared experiences was too thin to hold on. My race was run, and the season had changed. I no longer had the energy for forced interaction and jaded conversation. There was simply nothing more to share.

There are dark times in leaving familiarity behind. The fear of lost friendships and undiscovered new friends is terrifying. Initially, I felt a deep sense of loss, insecurity, and guilt.

Many sleepless nights were spent rewinding circumstances and questioning my decision to part ways. Good and bad memories mingled, usually leaving the bad memories to surface as a justifying excuse for the breakup. Triggers presented themselves everywhere: music we shared, places we visited, photos and laughs and tears. At the time, I wasn't brave enough to explain how I felt, as I thought it would only stimulate debate and hurt. I simply made excuses to not join their celebrations and faded away. They were confused and questioned my absence, but as I let go of that season of friendship and thought more intentionally about how I wanted to spend my time and most importantly with whom, I felt enormously relieved and at peace. From those feelings of peace, I chose carefully and surrounded myself with those I deeply love.

I still feel sad when I remember the good times. But when I bump into my old acquaintances on my weekly grocery trip, I no longer hide when I hear their voices in the adjacent aisle. I confidently walk up and am pleasantly kind.

They walk away content that they are not at fault.

I walk away with the knowledge that my soul is at peace, quietly thanking them for their part in my journey while valuing and appreciating each individual friend I now have in my circle, which is completely in tune with my soul.

* * * *

Julie decided to leave a circle of friends she no longer felt communion with. At first she judged and blamed them. She stayed within the group because it was a form of people-pleasing and living within what had come to be expected of her. But when Julie really examined all her thoughts and found the primary one was, "I want simpler friendships with shared values and deep conversations," it generated a feeling of peace. The circumstance didn't change, but her thoughts did, and that created different actions. She no longer hid when she heard her old friends because she decided she could love them without judging them and still like her reasons for moving away from them. This was a "good" bye.

Relationships will undoubtedly shift throughout the years, and sometimes there is great sadness in the dissolution of a friendship, partnership, or marriage. Making decisions will not prevent you from feeling. In fact, the opposite is true. You will feel a myriad of feelings when you are making changes. It is in the space of indecision that we go numb.

How often have you felt numb? I know I have when I chose not to feel sadness as if that were an unacceptable feeling. My clients often report feeling numb when they just cannot make a decision, often out of fear of what others will think. They suffer from numbness with a side of anxiety. These emotions become the daily diet despite the vast platter of available emotions from which they could choose.

DECISIONS INVOLVING MINORS

What about children? How do we make decisions on our own behalf when we also must consider our children? I'm not going to pretend it will be comfortable or without pain, but I am going to suggest that decisions made solely for the purpose of pleasing someone else will never be authentically satisfying or good for anyone. The intended outcome of keeping the peace and keeping everyone happy will not happen. You will be living a lie that is out of integrity, which will cause you to act in ways that will ultimately create the very situation you were attempting to avoid.

Let's say you want to leave your marriage but decide to stay for the children. Your thought is, "I don't want my children to suffer." But how will you act and show up each and every day if you stay in your marriage? Resentful, victimized, demanding that others make you happy because you've sacrificed to make them happy? Will you choose to make yourself suffer?

How will you know if your children are suffering? What will you teach them about their thoughts and feelings if they see you modeling that your thoughts and feelings aren't important? Taking care of your emotional adulthood by managing your thoughts and feelings is the best way to teach your children to find their own power and sovereignty. Even little children.

Asking the question, "Should I stay or go?" based on deciding who will suffer the most or the least is not the most valuable question. Perhaps it's better to ask, "How can I show myself love, caring, and support so that I have the love, caring, and support to give my children as we all navigate our changed family dynamics?"

When we manage our own thoughts and feelings, we realize we can experience any and all emotions, and that expands us. When we believe we are at the effect of another's actions, we relinquish our power. We are not at the effect of others, but at the cause for ourselves. In every situation we ultimately have the power to choose what we want to make something mean.

No one can make you happy, and no one can make you sad. These are all your feelings, and you are wholly responsible for them. There is no "one size fits all" answer, but working with a therapist or coach can be invaluable for helping you create awareness of what you are thinking and feeling so that you ultimately make decisions from integrity instead of fear.

THOUGHT GEM

JUST DECIDE to make a choice by asking yourself first if you like your choice.

PAUSE AND REFLECT

1. Are you currently struggling with a decision because you are trying to please someone else?

2. What would you decide if either (*a*) no one else was involved or (*b*) if the person(s) involved agreed with your decision?

3. Why is pleasing someone else more important?

4. What would you have to believe in order to support yourself and make the decision you want?

____

____

____

____

____

CHAPTER 6 WOULDA, COULDA, SHOULDA

"I never wanted to be the person who said, 'I woulda, coulda, shoulda.' Life is way too short, and you may not last that long."

~ Joy Bryant ~

So often we lament our past decisions by thinking about what we woulda, coulda, or shoulda done if only…. Here are some of the most recent "woulda, coulda, shoulda" comments my clients have shared:

"I wish I would've invested in Amazon when it was $172 a share instead of $3,700."

"If only I would've taken that job overseas instead of choosing the security of staying in my hometown, I'd be further along in my career."

"I should have chosen a better partner, so I wouldn't be divorced today."

"I could've avoided developing diabetes if only I managed my diet better."

We will discuss issues relating to the "wouldas" and "couldas" in greater detail in the next chapter, "Arguing with the Past," but for now, I want to focus on the "shouldas," which can be particularly difficult to navigate. Unlike the words "would" and "could," which imply willingness and capability, "should" suggests an inescapable obligation. When we talk about all the "shoulds" in our lives, like, "I should stay near my family. I should give up my job and become my mother's caregiver. I should not apply for the promotion and just be happy that I have a job. I should exercise more. I should stay in my relationship because I am too old to have another chance. I should take less so that others have more," we assault ourselves. This tyranny of shoulds is like "shoulding" on yourself: it's going to be messy and certainly stink.

The truth is you shouldn't do anything except take care of yourself because no one else will. Does that mean you should become a selfish, narcissistic, single-minded person? No, it's just meant to say that when you examine what you think you should do (e.g., take more time for yourself) and extrapolate from it the truth (e.g., that if you take some "me time" you will be replenished for your other responsibilities), you begin to make reasonable choices and don't feel the resentment of existing at the effect of a decision.

With this in mind, "I should take more time for myself" becomes "I get to enforce the idea that I need an hour alone each evening to take care of myself, which is awesome because I am as important a human being as the ones that I love, care for, work for, and pass on the street. I want to see myself in that way, and this is how I can make sure that happens."."

> *Stop shoulding on yourself.* Instead, identify what you want and why. Once you have, take pride in and responsibility for your choices.

LANGUAGE HACKS: WHAT YOU SAY MATTERS

As the examples above may suggest, often we are either unconscious or careless about our word choices. When I trained with Tony Robbins, one of the world's most renowned and influential personal development gurus, he asked us to make a list of the emotions we felt at least once a week. Although there are three thousand words to describe emotions, most people reported habitually feeling about five good feelings with the rest being negative. In fact, 90 percent of the people in the room wrote down an average of a dozen feelings, and more than half of those words described negative feelings. Robbins described this as a universal response he has seen over more than two decades, with audience sizes ranging from two thousand to thirty thousand people worldwide. With so much emphasis on negative emotion, is it any wonder depression is on the rise?

The question is, do we feel bad or worse *because* of the words we choose? Robbins examined the language patterns of different people and how those patterns either magnified or softened an emotion. He found words like "furious" or "enraged" had a different tone than "peeved" or "upset" and that each had different physiological outcomes. He proved words don't just describe our reality; they actually shape it. Thoughts are so powerful that Dr. Andrew Newberg and Mark Robert Waldman wrote about it in their book, *Words Can Change Your Brain.* Right down to the cellular level, the authors were able to scientifically prove that, "A single word has the power to influence the expression of genes that regulate physical and emotional stress."

Dr. Emoto, a Japanese scientist, performed unusual science experiments exploring how words might affect our physical bodies. He investigated how the physical molecular properties of water changed based on exposing it to a variety of words, thoughts, and sounds. He chose water because the adult human body is made of roughly 50 to 75 percent water, so in short he was investigating how our words may be affecting our physical bodies. Dr. Emoto exposed purified water to two different thought patterns and words: benevolent, compassionate, and loving versus fearful and negative thoughts. He used magnetic resonance analysis (MRA) and high-speed photography to observe microscopic changes in the water's crystalline configurations. Over a period of time, the frozen crystals exposed to loving words such as "love" and "gratitude" revealed brilliant, complex, and colorful snowflake patterns. In contrast, the water exposed to negative thoughts and words such as, "You disgust me" revealed incomplete, asymmetrical, dull patterns or in some cases a total absence of a crystal. You can see the photographs and read more in his fascinating book, *The Hidden Messages in Water.*

With so much evidence supporting the power of words and thoughts, consider these common expressions and see how shifting your thoughts with your word choices can change your feelings. Remember, the only way to change your actions is by changing your feelings. Notice how these various expressions impact your feelings.

SHOULD/NEED/MUST	WANT/GET TO	AM/HAVE
I should take care of my mother	I get to take care of my mother	I am taking care of my mother because I love her and want to.
I need more money	I want more money	I am creating more money
I must lose weight	I want to lose weight	I am choosing to do what's necessary to lose weight
I need a partner to be happy	I get to be happy by choosing to be happy	When I am happy, I more easily connect with my partner
I don't know how	I get to research this further	I can find the answer
I'm overwhelmed; there's too much to do	I always get to make a choice about what I do	I accept I am human and choose what I value and prioritize most
I'm stuck and confused	I get to make a choice	I will make a choice and learn

Once you get in the habit of reframing your negative "shoulds" into positive "get tos," the related decisions to take action, well, *should* get easier too.

THOUGHT GEM

Your words influence every cell in your body. JUST DECIDE to create the reality you want by choosing your words thoughtfully.

CHAPTER 7 ARGUING WITH THE PAST

"When you argue with reality, you lose, but only 100 percent of the time."

~ Byron Katie ~

I want to emphatically state that if you've experienced any type of abuse, trauma, or PTSD, it's best to consult a licensed psychologist or psychiatrist who is trained to help people safely deal with these issues that are beyond the domain and expertise of life coaching.

In the last chapter, I introduced the concept of the "wouldas, couldas, shouldas" as they apply to decision-making. Remorse, regret, and arguing with the past may seem like useful strategies for trying to make sense of situations, not to mention for trying to make decisions, and these behaviors fill the hours and paychecks of countless therapists, psychiatrists, counselors, and coaches around the world.

I'm not knocking any of these people. I myself am a coach and have spent more than my fair share of hard-earned money yammering about the past and arguing about why it shouldn't have been that way. But here's the thing. *It did happen that way.* Whatever it was... the man who dumped me, the baby I lost to miscarriage, the dad I couldn't save when he had a sudden heart attack and my CPR failed, the financial loss of 75 percent of my income in 2008 when the world sort of fell apart, the dear friends who died of cancer and car accidents, the torment of my bulimia, and my husband's alcoholism.... all of those things and more happened.

Just like in your life. In all of these circumstances, there was only one common thing that pulled me out, and that was asking myself, "What did I make it mean?" Trust me, it wasn't a quick thought swap from "This is horrible and devastating," to "I am so happy I got to learn so much from this." It was a process of consciously evaluating each of my thoughts repeatedly. I truly learned the value of that work when I was coaching a client who shared the traumatic event of discovering her ex-husband, who apparently had died alone three days earlier and hadn't been discovered until she found him. For a moment, I agreed with her thought that what she experienced was traumatic. I empathized with her while secretly thinking that I didn't know how I would have responded to that traumatic event. I thought, "I've never really suffered trauma," but when I thought of my own experience trying to revive my father from a sudden heart attack during dinner, I realized I no longer processed this as trauma.

You see, my initial thought about my father's death was that I had somehow failed him: "I wasn't good enough. I didn't do CPR well enough, and if I had done it right, he'd be alive." Talk about arguing with the past! My theme song of not being "good enough" permeated my life for the better part of my twenties, thirties, forties, and even fifties. Sure, I had a long list of accomplishments of which I was proud, but that fundamental feeling of not being good enough was deeply ingrained in my psyche. Not surprisingly, in my coaching practice, I see that feeling of inadequacy and "not good enough" as a common, if not universal, lament. In my own life, I will honestly say not-enoughness sometimes rears its scared head as a default thought, but I catch it now more quickly, notice it, and compassionately acknowledge it as if it's a well-meaning but confused individual, and when I struggle with the thought, I seek my own coaching. Even though I know my thoughts are not facts, they often feel so true. Coaches help us see our minds, our thoughts, and our blind spots. They help us come to the awareness that it's our thoughts, not the events, conditions, situations, or things someone else has done or said that cause pain.

Arguing with the past may taint our decision-making process because we bring all of our thoughts, feelings, and actions into the present with us. We might think, "If my husband hadn't lost his job, then I wouldn't have to go to work." "Losing my baby means I'll never get pregnant again, or it will be so hard that maybe I shouldn't even try." "If only I'd sold my house soon after we lost our income, then I wouldn't be draining my IRA now." "If only I held on to my house soon after we lost our income, then it would've been worth so much more today. I should have waited."

The truth about arguing with the past is that we will never win. No matter how much we rail against it, whatever cruel, horrible, unimaginable thing or circumstance occurred, no matter how much we didn't want it to happen and know, at the deepest level of our being, that it shouldn't have happened, the horrible reality is that whatever it was that happened *did happen*.

When we argue with the past, we double our grief, anger, guilt, and remorse. We feel our feelings about the actual event or circumstances and then exacerbate our suffering with feelings of frustration, anger, and resentment that it happened at all. Please do not interpret this to sound dismissive, uncaring, or unempathetic. In fact, allowing acceptance (even if it's in incremental stages) of what happened is the only way to free yourself from the draining energy of resistance.

There are, however, many instances in which we wish and believe something shouldn't have happened even though the reality is that it did. My client Bonnie contacted me several months after her twin brother suffered a stroke. She was his power of attorney and health advocate, in charge of everything from his medical care to his finances, because his brain injury rendered him legally incapable of making decisions and her brother had no spouse or children.

Bonnie was angry, sad, and scared. "He should've taken better care of himself and taken his medicines and exercised. He shouldn't live alone." According to Bonnie, her brother continued to be noncompliant in his nursing home and rejected Bonnie's loving suggestions to improve his physical condition. Bonne's brother labeled her as "controlling," and he often hung up on her when she called. Bonnie thought she was struggling because her brother had a stroke, but what really caused her suffering was her thinking, "It shouldn't have happened. I want to control this." As a result, she felt angry and scared, and from those feelings she tried to control the situation with different actions that alienated her brother even further. Ironically her actions actually prevented her from getting curious and asking her brother what he wanted, what was important to him, so that she could help him work toward achieving his outcomes. After a few sessions, Bonnie began to realize she had options in her thinking. Bonnie shared this story.

BONNIE'S STORY

I was standing in my kitchen, listening to my brother's doctor tell me I had to "let go." He elaborated. "At some point you're going to need to tell yourself: Stop. Just stop. And then—let it go. Let go."

My first reaction was, "Well, you may be well-informed from a medical point of view, but I am the one who knows my twin brother and loves and cares about my nearest and dearest sibling. So how can you give me this advice?"

And then I remembered my coaching sessions I had done just weeks before. We had discussed what I made it mean when I thought about my brother's stroke and how it shouldn't have happened. I saw how my thoughts had me arguing about events from the past that were... facts. Also from my coach I had learned about the self-help tool of "EFT tapping" that lowers our stress response so we can be more resourceful and make more deliberate decisions, and I had been tapping each morning as soon as I awoke. So in that moment I was able to be open to the possibility of thinking a different thought. My thinking was: "I am letting go, and (not but) I am not loving him any less." Instead, I stopped adding pain to my experience. Also, I leaned into my curiosity. I remember thinking intentionally, "I am being loving and curious and affectionately open to my future and to the needs of my brother."

* * * *

From this new place of curiosity and compassion, Bonnie engaged with her brother differently. She recognized the warm friendship he had established with one of his caregivers and began to observe what progress he was making toward his independence. Not too long after, her brother became self-sufficient enough to leave his skilled nursing care facility and return home to independent living. Bonnie learned to love her brother even if she didn't always agree with his choices, and their relationship once again became loving and communicative. She celebrated his success at his return to independent living by appreciating the meal he cooked for her when she visited him.

TRY THIS EXERCISE TO STOP ARGUING WITH THE PAST

Tell a story you've told before about your health, career, or relationships, but now tell it in two different ways. First, tell the story in a way where you focus on all the negative details. Next retell the same story, but edit it by extracting every detail that was wonderful. Your ability to edit your life's details will provide you with a story that has you either longing or learning, anguishing or affirming. Although we can't change the past, we can decide what we want to make it mean.

THOUGHT GEM

JUST DECIDE how you will retell the stories of your past.

8 CHAPTER WHAT DO YOU MAKE IT MEAN?

Things do not have meaning.
We assign meaning to everything.

~ Tony Robbins ~

When approaching any decision, asking the question, "What do I make it mean if I do this or think that?" creates the space for us to get curious. It is our thoughts that give everything meaning because our circumstances are always neutral. Our circumstances are neither good nor bad, right nor wrong, positive nor negative *until we have a thought about them*. Then we heap additional thoughts and judgment upon our thoughts, creating even more confusion. As previously mentioned, confusion is just a state of being that allows us to cycle in indecision. Confusion drains us of vital energy. It's like a toilet stuck in the flushing cycle, when it just keeps rushing water but it never completes its action. The shit's still there. It's a lot of action with no results.

The most critical part of making a decision is your mindset. Even before you work on any strategy, you must align your thoughts to believe that you will find a way, become decisive, and pull the trigger on the decision. This doesn't suggest you make a decision impulsively just to get the pain over with. It means having your own back, believing you are capable, and knowing the sense of gratification, not just relief, you will feel from actually deciding. *The ninja secret is deciding to decide.* For simplicity's sake, let's use the common analogy of driving. Think of your mindset like putting your key in the ignition and turning your car's engine on. This simple act tells your brain you are ready to go somewhere. Your engine is revved and waiting for you. You have broken through the most difficult part of inertia. In other words, you are committed to moving from where you are to where you want to be. When you move from park to drive, you have taken the next step, but unless you put your foot on the gas, you will remain where you are and drain all your gas and energy by being in neutral or stuck mode. When you put your foot on the gas pedal, that is your fuel. Your gas pedal is your emotional state. It is your feelings that fuel you to take actions, but of course everything started with the thought.

Speaking of thoughts, we tell the stories of our lives in such a way they could be *National Enquirer* headlines. While it is initially gratifying to get the story out in all its graphic detail, when we strip the stories down to just the facts, we can see and understand the true neutrality of the circumstance. If you are old enough to remember the TV show *Dragnet* from the late fifties and sixties, you'll remember Joe Friday, played by Jack Webb, the hardcore cop who methodically interrogated suspects and gathered facts about a case. He was a no-nonsense, don't-tell-me-a-story kind of guy, who became famous for saying, "Just the facts, ma'am."

For the most part, as we describe our own stories to ourselves or others, it's helpful to genuinely examine what is factual—that is, what could be proven in a court of law. Why this is important is because we have no control over circumstances. Things can and do happen, but where our power and agency for change occurs is in our thoughts and feelings. In other words, what we *make a circumstance mean* will lead to the feelings we have and the actions we take. We will review this basic premise in this book many times because it is not what we are accustomed to believing. We wholeheartedly believe our circumstances are causing the problem and that if they were different we would feel better. We are used to getting agreement from our friends or those who care about us when we relay circumstances and situations where we believe we've been wronged in some way: The jerk boyfriend who made a snide comment. The asshole boss who passed us over for a promotion. The rude driver who cut us off and caused us to crash into a pole. We believe if only we could change our husbands, partners, jobs, houses, our weight, or how much money we have, we would be happier and better off. While that looks true on the surface, what we are really changing when we change those things is our *thoughts* about the new things.

REFRAMING THE MEANING OF CIRCUMSTANCES AND DECIDING

We are taught to think based on cause and effect, a kind of "If ________________________, then________________________."

But when we examine the thoughts we have about our circumstances, we can see that multiple meanings are possible and that our outcomes are directly related to how we frame or in some cases reframe the meaning of those circumstances.

Listen to M.J.'s story in her own words about how she decided to view her health and reframe the meaning of her heart condition.

M.J.'S STORY

Ba-boom. Ba-boom. That's the rhythm of a regular heartbeat. If your heart beats normally you don't notice it, but the heart condition of extrasystoles feels different. Ba-boom-Baa. Pause. Ba-boom. Extrasystoles are additional heartbeats that occur outside the heart rhythm. When an extrasystole happens, it feels like a huge hit in your chest. It's alarming, and that's all you can think about. Some days, you might not have any or only one or two, but from time to time they can occur much more frequently.

Cardiologists generally tell you it's a benign arrhythmia that won't harm you unless it's really frequent or persistent. They tell you to relax and forget about them. Although this condition seems to be related to high levels of anxiety, neither psychiatrists nor cardiologists have further answers.

I started to feel mine ten years ago, when my kids were aged one and two and a half. I was exhausted, extremely skinny, and still breastfeeding my youngest. During that time, my beloved grandfather passed away unexpectedly. His death devastated me and triggered thoughts about how my heart disease would cause me to die young and leave my kids orphaned.

Even though imagining this worst-case scenario added to my stress and created a higher level of anxiety that worsened my problem, I didn't exactly know what to do about it, so I began working with a life coach and doing my own self-coaching because what I did know was that I wanted to feel better and in more control. I began exploring my own thoughts and questioned if my thoughts were facts or something my mind was catastrophizing. The biggest shift came when I realized I didn't have to believe my heart condition could kill me. I could actually decide what experiencing extrasystoles meant. My first thought shift was, "These will not kill me," and while that was an improvement, I still definitely thought, "It is hard to live with these extrasystoles." Thinking that made me feel depressed because I still didn't think I had any choice or power. I noticed that when I felt depressed I stopped doing things. I didn't even want to spend time with my kids.

* * * *

When M.J. clearly saw the full impact of how her thoughts created her feelings and led to her actions, she realized she was inadvertently creating what she feared the most: a situation in which she was orphaning her children even while she was alive.

M.J. CONTINUES HER STORY...

My problem was not the extrasystoles, but what I thought about them. I decided to tell myself: "I can live with them." It might seem silly, but I decided to borrow my thoughts about hiccups, which could be considered a similar experience to a certain extent. At first, it didn't feel believable to me, but I kept thinking that thought, and one day, I just realized those were my new beliefs and I didn't have to talk myself into it.

Everything changed for me. The extrasystoles still come and go, and I don't expect them to disappear. But when I feel them, I'm not scared or downcast any more. I go on with my life almost as if they were not there.

* * * *

M.J.'s heart condition didn't change, but by reframing the meaning of those extrasystoles, she created a different reality and life experience for herself. Today she enjoys an active life with her growing children, including reviving her decades-long passion of horseback riding, even embracing the adrenaline rush of galloping. M.J. says, "I am so happy. It's something I thought I could never dare to dream, and here I am living the life I choose!"

M.J. understands the power of thoughts so much so that she's become a coach helping others who share her heart condition.

Before we practice factually writing the details of our problem or circumstance, I've provided a few examples of *incorrectly* written circumstances that are the *National Enquirer* version of circumstances; that is, full of *thoughts*, not facts. Words that are underlined reveal subjective, not factual, information. Then, I follow up with more factual ways of rephrasing and reframing the situation. Read them both and consider which would put you in a clearer frame of mind to make a decision.

Job Circumstance:

I am **overworked** at my job and don't get **properly** compensated. My boss demands I work **overtime** and **expects** that I **always** change my schedule to accommodate her needs.

Factually Written Job Circumstance:

1. I work eighty hours a week and am paid for sixty hours.
2. My boss said, "You need to work on Saturday."

Financial Circumstance:

My partner **lied** about an **investment** he made that **lost us money**, and so we **couldn't** pay for our son's college tuition at the school he wanted to go to.

Factually Written Financial Circumstance:

1. My partner invested $30,000 in a friend's startup, which is now worth $10,000.
2. We have $10,000 to pay for our son's college tuition.

Relationship Circumstance:

I am **certain** my husband is **cheating**. He says he has "work meetings" and comes home at midnight every Tuesday smelling of perfume.

Factually Written Relationship Circumstance:

1. My husband is away from home from 8:00 a.m. until midnight every Tuesday. When he comes home, he states, "I had a work meeting." He smells of perfume that is not mine.

In this last example, I get that you might be rolling your eyes and thinking, "Why would I give the bastard a pass? If it looks like a duck and smells like a duck, it must be a duck."

Whether it's a goose, duck, whatever, the point of making something factual is to remind ourselves that the situation is neutral until we have a thought about it. When we can curiously look at a situation, we expand our ability to take action from a place of clarity, alignment, and integrity.

Like M.J., you will get better at this reframing as you practice, but for now, do your best to replicate the simplicity of the factual circumstances given above with your own circumstance. Remember to use a single sentence to describe the problem.

Use the workbook to write out the facts of your situation. To make it clean, put the circumstance or situation into a single sentence.

PAUSE AND REFLECT

Let's work on making your problem factual.

1. What decision are you currently struggling with?

____

____

____

____

____

____

2. Practice making it factual. Rephrase any thought- or emotion-based language into factual statements.

____

____

____

____

____

____

THOUGHT GEM

JUST DECIDE that your circumstances aren't the problem. It's what you make them mean that ultimately influences your decisions about how to manage them.

SECTION III

REDECIDING YOUR FUTURE

In the previous section you learned that your past should remain in the past and that your future should be created with only your future in mind. In this next section the following chapters will have you actively "Re-Deciding Your Future" by examining your present and deliberately deciding what's next in your life. You'll bust through the fears of making the wrong decision and learn what it takes to make the best decision. These exercises will teach you how to regret-proof your decisions while curating your exquisite bespoke life.

9 CHAPTER DO YOU WANT WHAT YOU HAVE?

"It's not having what you want, it's wanting what you've got."

~ Sheryl Crow ~

Read that chapter title again. Your eyes and brain will generally default to the question that's most commonly asked, which is "What do you want?" not "Do you want what you [already] have?"

There are material wants (e.g., a house, a car, a relationship, a bank account with a million dollars) and there are "state of being" wants or "emotional feeling" wants (e.g., peace, curiosity, energy, excitement). We frequently don't put feelings on our wish list or our goal list when deciding what we want, and we often don't notice if what we are currently feeling is what we want to feel on purpose. We generally assume that our emotional states are as unpredictable as the weather and that our emotional fluctuations are entirely dependent on our circumstances, the events and conditions of our experiences. But as I've referenced many times in this book, all of our power is in our thoughts.

What if every major decision we've made required an annual, mandatory renewal agreement to check in and see if that's still what we want and what is in harmony with our current self?

We change, we evolve, we grow, and things or circumstances, such as relationships, residences, and lifestyle choices, should be regularly considered as new and fresh. Would we *want* what we have? So often when a person is asked what they want, the reply is not about what they currently have, as if all wanting is in the future and heretofore unattained. If you asked yourself, "Do I want what I have in my relationship, my choice of job, my friendships, my clothes in my closet, the food that I choose?" what might you answer?

The point isn't to jump ship and go for what's perceived to be the new, shiny object or to assume that your circumstances are not making you happy. The intention isn't actually to change the circumstance but to examine your thoughts about the circumstances. This redeciding is somewhat like a forest fire that comes through and burns a fresh forest field to allow for new growth.

Wanting what we have is a beautiful thing. Wanting what we have means saying, "Yes, I would choose that again because it's consistent with my values and thoughts." It's different than having what you want, which ignores the thing and puts it in a lifeless, unappreciated state. This distinction is so important to consider before leaving anything or quitting anything. This process of deciding to want what you have is a thoughtful examination of what you have and why you wanted it in the first place.

When I was first asked where I would be in five, ten, or twenty years, I was truly stumped as if I would not be the one deciding. When I asked the question, "What do I want to be, do, or have?" and narrowed the time frame from five years down to five months, five days, and five hours, I started to hone in on what I valued and really wanted. That exercise done in my twenties still rings true today for my top three things in my sixties: to be physically and mentally healthy and fit, to be in a committed, loving relationship with my spouse/family, and to travel the world.

When someone says, "I have no idea where life will take me in twenty years," it's not entirely accurate. Life doesn't take you. You take your life wherever you go. Your decisions or indecisions are those very footsteps that take you where you are headed.

What do you want? What seems like a simple question often provokes the most agonizing and self-critical response. When clients say, "I don't know," not only do they struggle with the not knowing part, but they judge themselves for being so dumb or surprised or hopeless that they are forty, fifty, sixty, or even seventy and *should* know the answer but don't. If this resonates with you, you are not alone. This blank slate of not knowing doesn't mean there is something wrong with you; it simply means you've never allowed yourself to give up the resistance of not knowing to explore the processes of knowing and deciding. The truth is you've had whispers and glimpses and inspirations that have tickled your impulses, but likely you've squashed those thoughts with other thoughts and limitations before any one of them could sprout just the tiniest leaves of creation.

Having what we want and wanting what we have is often ignored, but awareness of this concept is so central to one's ability to recognize satisfaction. Most people believe that the key to feeling and being satisfied comes from changing their conditions, but the reality is first we must change our thoughts. We cannot get to the place of having more money by thinking about how little we have and how much everyone else has. This mindset of scarcity and lack causes feelings of disappointment, anger, and shame, which never lead one to take actions that would generate wealth. *You must first want what you* ***already*** *have to get what you don't* ***yet*** *have.*

I was working with my client Sheila, who was unsatisfied with her current "part-time fill-in job," a job she took after being laid off and feeling terrified that she'd have no income since she was a divorced woman in her late fifties. I asked her, "Do you want what you have?"

Her response was, "No, this job is just filling time until I get a real job."

She wasn't wrong in being dissatisfied. It made sense since her thought was, "This isn't a real job; I'm just filling in time," which caused her to feel dissatisfied. Feeling dissatisfied permeated her state of mind and showed up in the way she marginally performed her work. Yes, she fulfilled her duties, but she did so in a perfunctory way to get the job done. The effect of her "filling time" limited her own potential. She was putting herself on hold while blaming it on the circumstances. No one could say whether or not a better job existed at that company, but ultimately whatever you do, I told Sheila, you do for yourself. If you show up with energy, enthusiasm, and a work ethic that reflects your level of integrity, whether you're washing toilets or creating billion-dollar software, you are the ultimate benefactor because energetically you are "wanting what you have." Wanting what you have doesn't limit you. There is no chance of getting stuck because you are *not* dissatisfied. You can't achieve "wanting more" from the place of *not wanting what you have.* You must energetically match the vibration of what you want. You have to create the welcome conditions to be prepared and in alignment with the energy you want in the future.

Why is wanting what you have important to decision-making? Because you will so often be tempted to make a decision based on thinking you will be happier *over there,* as if the new circumstances could provide you with happiness. A decision made from a place of discontent with the expectation that something outside of yourself will make you happier will generally lead to disappointment. When we choose a new mate, job, or house with the expectation that that thing or change will make us happier, we hand over all our power to that external thing. Should that mate leave us or we lose our job, we can end up feeling victimized. As a culture we are used to thinking, "If I do or get X, *then* I will be happy." In reality, we only do things because of how we think doing those things will make us feel. But the incredible secret is we can cultivate whatever feeling we want in advance of getting that thing. When you decide that how you feel is entirely up to you, you discover enormous power.

The new logic goes like this:

"I'll be happy, and *then* ____________________" versus "I'll be happy *when* ____________________."

The first time I heard this concept from Brooke Castillo of *The Life Coach School,* I balked at the idea. My initial thought was, "Wait, what?" If I was comfortable with where I was or who I was with or where my finances were or where I lived, then why in the heck would I want to change things? I considered this idea very thoughtfully when I was struggling in my then thirty-year marriage.

MY PERSONAL STORY

From about year twenty-six of my marriage and well into our thirtieth year together, our relationship began to have stress marks that turned into fractures that chipped away at anything that tied us together. Holding on felt more like an endurance contest than a marriage.

The long-term communication problems we had were further strained by the financial challenges of losing 75 percent of our income in 2008. My husband wasn't responsible for this loss. His compensation and our life's savings were largely based on the stock his company gave him, but this stock was restricted, meaning he couldn't sell it even though it was plummeting. We just had to watch our net worth disintegrate. My then sixty-one-year-old husband's management position was eliminated, and although he wasn't fired, he didn't have a job. Up till this point he'd done an excellent job of making investments and making sure our IRAs were growing. We had a cushion for this emergency, so we decided to stay in our home thinking our finances would improve, but after three years of draining our IRAs to make the house payments, we finally sold our home and moved into a rental that allowed my teenage daughter to complete high school with her friends. Apart from the stunning view, the rental was dilapidated and dysfunctional and a daily reminder (in my husband's mind) of his financial collapse. He lapsed into several months of deep depression, with feelings of loss, shame, and a shaken faith in his skills and his future.

Eventually he genuinely overcame his limiting beliefs and cultivated a new idea for a partnership with two other colleagues. The creation process was fun, challenging, and a big investment of money, emotional commitment, and time. The partnership, however, eventually dissolved through a series of disagreements and failures among all parties to come to the same conclusion and understanding of events. This loss led to a longer, deeper level of depression, resistance, and an ever-widening gap between us.

My husband was truly hurting. He was loyal and committed to our relationship and to his self-expectation of being a provider for the family. My expectations for him were that he should view things more positively with hope and belief. I thought it wasn't fair to live with someone who was depressed. I reasoned if only he would stop feeling guilt and shame he could find a way to create wealth and abundance. I had lots of ideas about what he should do and feel. In the meantime

I gathered "evidence" of why our marriage was failing, why he wasn't the right partner for me, why I had made the wrong choice, and why at the age of sixty I should consider leaving and getting "one last chance at life." I'd convinced myself and my supportive friends that I deserved better and could be happier. I even went so far as to copy all of our financial statements without my husband's knowledge, find a divorce attorney, and consult with others who'd gone through divorces. I considered where I'd live and how I would dissolve my relationship. I mentally rehearsed the conversation I'd have with our college-aged daughter hundreds of times. Although I tried to understand the concept of neutral circumstances, I didn't believe my circumstances were neutral. I was certain I was right and that our marriage had run its course. I stacked all the evidence of all the difficulties and disagreements of our marriage to build a definitive case as to why I should leave. I wanted my husband to change so I would feel better. The reality was I wanted to leave because I desperately wanted to stop hurting.

You might wonder, "Isn't that a good enough reason?" It might be for some, but I urge you to consider the adult version of dealing with life's circumstances and processing pain. As long as I thought someone else was causing my pain, I was a victim. When I truly understood it wasn't my husband's depression that caused my suffering, but rather my thoughts about why life shouldn't be that way, that was the moment I found some leverage on my thoughts. It wasn't my job to fix him any more than it was his job to fix my annoying optimism. My job was to focus on myself and to manage my own mind instead of trying to manipulate his. I added unnecessary suffering to our relationship, but I didn't see it that way in my self-righteous thoughts of how good I was.

The most revelatory insight I had when considering leaving my marriage was that I'd be taking the current version of me to what I fantasized would be a better relationship. But that "me," if I was honest, was petty, judgmental, critical, and controlling. I began to realize that my true power simply lay within the thoughts I chose. When I shifted my focus toward managing my own mind and I stopped trying to manage my husband's thoughts, feelings, and behaviors, not so surprisingly our lives began to improve. Although we continued to share our finances equally, I decided I wanted to resume control of my own bank accounts, something I had willingly relinquished thirty years before when we married. I simply wanted to assume more responsibility and independence.

The urgency for divorce slowly dissipated. I began to notice all the ways that divorce would negatively affect the outcomes I desired, and more importantly that the real growth was my personal evolution. I focused more on myself and began to explore different work options that increased my self-confidence and finances. I began working full-time in the field of speech pathology, again earning double what I'd earned in previous years. I committed to my coaching business, which grew slowly but steadily, and I wrote and published my first book, ***Hope After Stroke For Caregivers and Survivors: The Holistic Guide to Getting Your Life Back****, which became an international bestseller and helped thousands of stroke survivors and their families find meaning and recovery after stroke.*

My husband was hugely supportive of the new me that was emerging. He willingly prepared meals and took on the many daily life chores so that I could write and coach. I started to look at him differently. Instead of seeing everything that was missing, including that which I was not giving, I also started seeing all the things I loved about him, including his generosity toward and encouragement of my new goals. We began to talk more and dream more about our long-term plans, and we shared a profound bonding experience on a trip to Africa. At the writing of this book we are celebrating our thirty-fifth wedding anniversary. Is everything "perfect"? Of course not, because we are human and humans are not perfect unless they're dead. But if and when I get frustrated, I examine my thoughts and the story I'm telling myself. I know the work always begins with my thoughts, and I recommit to managing my own mind.

* * * *

READER NOTE

Stories and anecdotes are meant to illustrate the various ways people have chosen to deal with a myriad of issues including marital, financial, and career decisions. There is no one right way or answer. As always, it is your thoughts that will generate your feelings and cause you to take the actions that create your results.

CULTIVATING THE FEELINGS TO APPEAL TO WHAT YOU WANT

Derek Rydall, a spiritual leader and the author of *Emergence: Seven Steps for Radical Life Change,* talks about "the polar bear concept." He says if you want a polar bear to come live with you and you live in the Arizona desert, you must create the conditions that will welcome him and allow him to survive. The same is true for any goal you create for yourself. You need to create the conditions in which your realized goal can thrive.

If you are dissatisfied with where you are in a relationship, a job, or a place of residence, the first step isn't to leave. The first step is to create satisfaction (i.e., the welcoming conditions right where you are), and this feeling state is fueled by—guess what? Our thoughts! We create the feelings we want by choosing the deliberate thoughts we want.

I hear you. How can we choose airy-fairy thoughts when what we feel is hate, revulsion, fear, disbelief, and doubt? We can't always jump in with a soothing affirmation like, "I am rich and have all the money I need for the rest of my life," especially when we don't believe it. Unless we actually believe our thoughts, we will reject even the most beautifully crafted affirmation. So how do we begin to cultivate believable thoughts to move us along the path from where we are to where we want to be?

Brooke Castillo coined the term "bridge and ladder" thoughts as a means to enable us to inch or bridge our way toward a shift in thinking that bypasses the immediate "Reject" button.

Take, for instance, the affirmation: "I have all the money I need for the rest of my life." If that causes you to launch into a rant citing evidence of the thousands of dollars of debt you have, how you live from paycheck to paycheck, how the cable company is threatening to disconnect you, you can start with these thoughts: "Money and wealth exist. More than one person has money. People have gotten out of debt. It's possible to get out of debt and be financially stable."

One can begin to ask the question, "What would a woman who had all the money she needed for the rest of her life feel? What thoughts would she be thinking that would cause her to feel secure, comfortable, and certain?"

If it's too hard to cultivate the feeling state on this topic because your brain rejects every plausible feeling with the thought, "Of course she feels that way because she has money," then begin to think of other situations completely unrelated to money where you feel certain, secure, and comfortable. Maybe you feel certainty, security, and comfort in a relationship with your friends or close family members. Maybe you feel those feelings in relation to your cat. Maybe you feel certain and secure in how your body functions, or perhaps you feel certain and secure in some area, no matter how small or seemingly insignificant, where you have already cultivated these feelings. Certainly the relationships we have with our pets provide that opportunity of unconditional love where we feel certainty, security, and comfort. Breathe into that space and feel the vibration of those feelings circulating within you. What are the thoughts you are thinking that trigger the feelings of safety, security, and comfort?

Now we're going to put those feelings into practice.

PAUSE AND REFLECT

Use the *workbook* to actually examine what your current feelings are about decisions you are contemplating.

What is a decision you want to make? It can be about your life, health, career, relationships, or even a decision to travel or make a purchase.

Let's examine your feelings.

What are you feeling? List all the different feelings you might have, including excitement and worry, uncertainty, guilt, etc.

Fill in the grid first by identifying your feeling in the column on the right. Then go back and fill in the grid with the simple thought that is triggering that feeling.

THOUGHT	FEELING

This next exercise may appear unusual, but it's all about moving energy. We know we are energetic beings. All we have to do is look at any of our standard medical tests like EKG and EEG readings that measure energy movements in our hearts and brains to know we have energy fields within us. This exercise is taken from the powerful practice of Neurolinguistic Programming (NLP), which is a very effective tool for rewiring the brain. NLP does this by creating powerful, quick, but deeply lasting cognitive and behavioral changes that utilize the power of our sensory brain, which encodes and stores all the information we receive from our senses.

We will do this in two parts. The first part is to activate a feeling state, and the second part is to get the energy to move in the direction that amplifies it. You will get to see how you can change your energy states with your senses.

To prepare for this exercise, you must imagine you are at a control center where you have the ability to amplify the sights, sounds, tastes, and smells you experience as if you had a control dial, so to speak. Imagine that the simple act of turning the dial would make the sensory experiences stronger or weaker depending on which way you turned it, just like any typical volume control dial on a radio.

1. Find somewhere you can relax and be comfortable, where you will not be disturbed.
2. With your eyes closed, think of a time when you felt wonderful.
3. Step into that memory. See the things you saw, hear the things you heard, smell the smells, and feel the feelings. Notice if the picture is in black and white or color. Is the picture close or far from you? Is the picture moving or still?
4. Intensify those sights, sounds, and feelings. Make them bigger, brighter, stronger, nearer. Experiment with which changes make the sensations feel even better. Find a point where everything is maximized.
5. Where in your body do you feel this good sensation? Trace this good sensation as it moves through you.
6. Amplify good feelings by making the movement bigger, stronger, and faster until you are bathed all over in this good feeling.
7. When you begin to amplify those feelings as if you have a volume dial that can turn up the intensity of everything you see, feel, smell, touch, and taste, then begin to use your finger to circle around your abdomen. Experiment with moving the energy in a clockwise rotation and feel whether that amplifies the good feeling or weakens it. Now reverse the rotation so you are circling around in a counterclockwise motion. Make the images bigger, brighter, more vivid and energetic.
8. Now, at the peak of this experience, touch your pinky finger to your thumb to anchor this feeling. Make sure to hold the fingers together only long enough that the feeling is truly at its peak intensity and then release. You've just created a "resource anchor."

9. The resource anchor you've just created is an association put into the context of a "trigger." We are triggered (unconsciously) all the time. Advertisers know this and utilize this basic human trait to influence and sell us products. We see a beautiful woman with perfect skin, and the cream she is using is anchored into our brains such that we make an association that this cream = beauty = a must-have. We smell apple pie baking, and we are triggered to remember our grandmother and the kitchen table we ate at with her. We hear a song, and we are instantly transported back to the relationship and time we were in when we first heard it.
10. 10. You can repeat this triggering of the anchor by simply touching the pinky and thumb together many times to recreate the experience of the feeling state. You may need to do it multiple times to create the cause-and-effect phenomenon and to make it significant enough that it is truly anchored. If you think back to any of the anchors you unconsciously created, you'll recognize that there were strong feelings and sensory experiences that created that anchor.

Practice, patience, and repetition will help you stabilize that anchor and enable you to achieve that feeling state more easily the more often you do it.

THOUGHT GEM

JUST DECIDE to ***want*** what you ***already*** have in order to get what you don't ***yet*** have.

CHAPTER 10 FEAR OF MAKING THE WRONG DECISION

"The risk of a wrong decision is preferable to the terror of indecision."

~ Maimonides ~

Fear of making the wrong decision is by far the single most driving thought that causes people to freeze in their tracks, delay decisions, and spiral into a black hole of inaction.

We believe that there must be a right decision and that if we don't make it, all will be lost. The stakes are so high, the fear is so great, and we are so convinced that there will be catastrophic, irrevocable consequences from which we will never recover if we make the wrong decision.

We've already talked about the cost of indecision, but there is also the cost of making a decision. Don't panic, we'll review the costs so you can anticipate and plan for them.

Just like with indecision, the cost of making a decision can fall into the following three categories:

The Emotional Cost

The Financial Cost

The Physical Cost

THE EMOTIONAL COST

The emotional cost of decisions simply means asking yourself, "How will I feel when I make this decision? Will I be happy? Scared? Irritated? Frustrated?" But the funny thing is most people don't spend enough time asking themselves how they will feel once they make a decision; instead they anticipate how others will feel.

As introduced in Chapter 5, "People Pleasing," we ruminate over whether we will be liked or criticized and judged for our decisions. Will our decisions affect someone else, causing them to feel happy, angry, afraid, annoyed, depressed, nervous, or vindictive?

For starters, have you ever noticed it's hard enough to control your own emotional state, let alone to try to control another's? Try as we might, we cannot control our children's, spouse's, boss's, friends', or parents' emotional states.

You might think you can make others happy by choosing one thing over another, but the reality is everyone can and will choose their own feelings based on what they make the circumstance mean. Trying to control their feelings will only exhaust you.

The emotional cost of a decision is measured in both the short term and the long term. If you're the guardian of your children, you're familiar with making decisions based on their long-term happiness. You set bedtime schedules despite them wanting to stay up till all hours. You choose food that nourishes them versus succumbing to their every cry to eat candy, chips, and junk food. You enforce that they go to school and complete their homework despite their protests and defiance. You do this because you have a long-term view of how to guide their lives. Yes, even during these times you might question things or relent simply because you can't take your child's whining and protests anymore. Your desire to make *your* pain stop is what you call "giving in." In reality, doing so does give you some short-term relief, but like most things that give us short-term relief, it often makes us feel worse later. We then get judgmental about our parenting skills and might feel resentful toward others for succumbing to manipulation, even though we made the choice. If you're like me, you might go down a deeper rabbit hole of what the perfect parent should think or do. At the core of your parenting, however, you know that, despite emotional protests and periods of deep unhappiness, defiance, and generalized snarkiness, you are at the helm of your children's journey and you are guiding them. Long-term happiness is ultimately created by delaying gratification, disciplining your mind to manage things and become self-reliant and capable.

I worked with the mother of an autistic child, Adam, who was fearful and worried about making a decision regarding her son's school placement. Her primary concern was having him feel accepted because she suffered when he'd cry, complaining that he didn't have friends and that school was too hard. A recommendation was made to place him in a special education classroom, in which his classmates would be functioning academically and emotionally more like he was. The school promised he'd receive a simplified curriculum in a much smaller class with professionals trained to work with special ed students. At the time, Adam was mainstreamed into an elementary school where he was a fifth grader functioning at the level of a first-grade student. In reality his peers did reject him because his maturity level was so different. His mother struggled with her decision, constantly repeating the thought, "I don't want to make the wrong decision for him." Because she was so fearful of making the wrong decision (though the decision was revocable), she made no decision at all.

In the short term, this allowed her to not fear the consequences of her decision, but by deciding not to decide, she left Adam to attend a large, regular middle school where he constantly left the classroom, cried, didn't form relationships with new friends, and did not get any academic support because he refused to stay in class. In reality, the very thing his mother feared would happen actually did happen. For six months she struggled with her son's unhappiness and the additional burden of her self-judgment that she was harming her son by not deciding. When she finally decided to move him to the other setting, Adam began to thrive. He even began to show his leadership skills and slowly began to establish friendships. In the long term, then, the emotional cost of her decision was negligible, if it existed at all.

THE FINANCIAL COST

This is the monetary price we pay for decisions, whether it's an investment, a car, a home, a piece of art or jewelry, the cost of leaving a marriage and hiring a divorce attorney, or the cost of schooling and paying for tuition. Most would agree that these are big risks, hefty costs that we think could financially devastate us if we make the "incorrect" decision. It's common that financial costs are fraught with evidence of all the past "errors" and mistakes we've made. Have I spent money on things I initially regretted but have since decided to reframe as learning experiences? Yes. In fact, I have made many decisions throughout my life that provided valuable chances to learn. However, now as I evaluate financial decisions, I apply the strategies I am sharing with you. Believing that money spent will never again materialize is a *thought*. A powerful and dangerous thought, yes, but it's an *optional* thought. Most people disagree; I know I did. I was so certain that taking a risk financially would be my last chance ever. Over time, I learned to appreciate the thought: "It's true, this money will never again be here, but there is always more money to create." I think this in the same way I consider that, "This food that I eat will never again be here, but I will always have food to eat."

The deeply powerful and ingrained scarcity mindset that creates the thought that money spent is gone forever is a self-limiting concept that exists only in our minds. I'm not suggesting one assume the complete opposite, a gambler's mindset. The gambler is not operating out of a mindset of abundance. They, too, are operating out of fear and scarcity, though their actions look quite different. They are always willing to risk everything because they believe their problems will be solved with one lucky draw. It's an addictive thrill that gives a sense of false pleasure and false security and almost always ends in a negative outcome.

There is the cost of *not spending* money to invest in yourself, too, whether it is avoiding the cost of an education, training, personal development, or even health care. Personally I've invested tens of thousands of dollars in my education, personal development, coaching, and health. The return on each of those investments has always been exponentially greater than their initial costs. An abundance mindset considers the value of something, not the cost, when it comes to making a decision.

I've learned to recognize value and benefit when making decisions. I've also learned to distinguish the feeling of wanting immediate gratification from knowing the value of long-term growth. Intuitively these feel different. There is urgency for wanting immediate gratification, whereas investing in something that requires me to grow feels expansive and activates feelings of certainty and determination. Every time I've said yes to spending money on a deeply desired opportunity for growth or travel, some "serendipitous" and unexpected money jettisoned into my life, like the former client from twenty years earlier who moved to Italy but found and hired me to coach him by phone or the speaking gig that suddenly appeared and paid me double the cost of the program I'd just joined. The point is, when you commit to your "Yes", the Universe conspires to support you. What are you not spending money on that you know would launch you forward into growth and possibilities? Decide now and invest in yourself.

THE PHYSICAL COST

There can often be a physical cost associated with a decision, especially when it comes to our health decisions. Seemingly small decisions of what to eat or not eat create either small or big consequences in our overall health. A diabetic who decides to eat whatever she wants runs the risk of long-term consequences of unmanaged high blood sugar, resulting in devastating consequences ranging from blindness to amputation to a diabetic coma to name just a few.

Decisions about wearing sunscreen and hats can create a physical cost, from something as manageable as a precancerous growth to something as devastating and lethal as melanoma.

There is the physical cost of staying in an abusive relationship where your physical safety is threatened; the physical cost of driving too fast because you are fueled with rage and you don't stop at a red light; the physical cost of overdrinking or overeating because you're avoiding decisions.

Ultimately decision-making or rather the lack of making a decision all boils down to one simple word and feeling: *fear.* We are afraid to make the wrong decision, yet the irony is we are already experiencing what we fear the most because not making a decision *is* the only wrong decision and surely the one that reinforces the proof that we don't know how to make one in the first place.

PAUSE AND REFLECT

1. Describe a decision you made (or didn't make) that had either an emotional, financial, or physical cost to you. If you want to dive deeper, you can do it for all three categories.

____

____

____

____

____

2. What valuable lesson can you extract from the outcome of the decision made?

____

____

____

____

3. Knowing what you now know, what, if anything, would you do differently? Why?

____

____

____

____

WHEN THE RIGHT DECISION FEELS WRONG

The truth is that some decisions will cause you to feel terrible even if they are the unequivocally "right" decision. Even decisions made with conviction and clarity don't guarantee that we'll feel good. After making the right decision, you may feel truly awful.

MY STORY

I was the medical advocate for my mother, tasked with enforcing her advance medical directive. This meant I needed to uphold her decision to "not prolong her life with extraordinary measures should a medical crisis occur." I was called upon to make that decision just four years after my father's sudden death. My dad suffered a heart attack in a restaurant during a family celebration, and my attempts to resuscitate him failed. What started as a joyful reunion turned into a series of decisions about funerals and obituaries.

Four years later, on Father's Day, I received a call from my cousin. I was living in New York City at the time, and my mother, who was sixty-four, was visiting my aunt and cousins in Ohio. They were headed to the pool when my mom suddenly collapsed. By the time paramedics arrived, she was in full cardiac arrest. My cousin called, telling me the ambulance had rushed my mom to the hospital and she was still in the emergency room. Nurses and doctors continued to attempt to revive her with compressions and cardiac stimulation even though she'd been unresponsive for forty-five minutes. The doctor offered grim predictions about the severe brain damage and complete disability my mother would likely suffer. They knew I was my mother's advocate. They wanted a decision. They asked me if I wanted to stop CPR for my mother. My immediate thought was, "I am being asked to make the decision to allow my mother to die." She was my last surviving parent. This thought terrified me. How could I know if it was right? How could I be responsible for my mother's death? I agonized over making that decision because I thought, "I will be the one responsible for my mother's death."

My mother designated me and trusted me to fulfill her decisions in the event she was unable to because she knew I had enough medical knowledge to ask questions and consider the decision rationally. She trusted me with her deeply personal decision. She believed I could rise to the occasion of adult maturity and enact her wishes should she become unable to advocate for herself. I knew what she wanted; we'd talked about death, disability, and "end of life" issues many times. We agreed on our definitions of quality of life and independence. I knew what I would want if I put my trust in someone else to fulfill my wishes. I clearly knew my decision, and yet it was awful, shocking, and came with a great deal of resistance. I had to make absolutely certain my mother's condition was so grave that it met her criteria of disability. My mother had no desire to live in a nursing home and be cared for if she couldn't walk or talk or eat on her own. I knew my decision was irrevocable. I knew my decision meant that as soon as physicians stopped performing CPR, my mother would be lost to me, my siblings, and the world forever. I knew I made the right decision because it was to fulfill my mother's ultimate wishes, but it was the hardest, most gut-wrenching decision of my life, and that was because I made it about me. The truth was it wasn't even my decision; it was only my promise to fulfill my mother's decision.

When I finally shifted my thoughts to realize my mother had chosen me to make this decision for her, I came to peace. Of course I grieved her loss and felt terribly sad, but I didn't torment myself with the thought that I was the one who stopped her life.

* * * *

THERE ARE NO WRONG DECISIONS

How can it be that there are no wrong decisions? All one has to do is look at world history or today's news and decide that there are endless numbers of pretty bad, wrong, terrible, no-good, horrible decisions. The decision to kill someone or steal or drive drunk or have sex with a minor; the decision to cheat or lie or harm someone else are all choices. It is our thoughts about them that make them right or wrong. I repeat: It is our thoughts about them that make them right or wrong. Humans are given free will to decide things, and that includes accepting the consequences of those decisions.

Is it semantics to say there are no good or bad decisions? Isn't that what Shakespeare said in *Hamlet*? "There is nothing either good or bad, but thinking makes it so." This concept is actually the basis of Cognitive Behavioral Therapy. It's true that every decision carries with it a consequence, but not all consequences are the same for each person. Perhaps a better question to ask is "Knowing the consequences of my decision, will I choose it?" Herein lies the conundrum. You may not know if you'll like the consequence until you've made the decision. There are some things, however, you automatically know. I know, for example, I would not like the consequence of drug or alcohol addiction. I've decided I like a clear mind and control of my body. I've decided in advance that I like my freedom and that means I pay my taxes. I've decided I get to go to work to contribute and that in turn provides me with income. I've decided to take care of my child because I love her and want to.

The point is all decisions are made either consciously or unconsciously, deliberately or unintentionally. The trouble is most of our lives we are making choices and decisions by default as if there were no choice.

If you're feeling frustrated by this philosophical pondering, now is a good time to look at decisions you've made or those you routinely make, the ones you choose consciously and the ones that you've never questioned and are automatic. If there are no bad decisions but thinking makes it so, how can you reframe your thoughts about your decisions or else change your decisions to get away from the feeling that they are "bad' or "wrong"?

IS THERE A RIGHT DECISION?

Decisions are neither right nor wrong until we have a thought about them. Otherwise, there is only a decision. We get to make any decision based on what we think about it, and in reality we get to decide if it was right or not.

Take, for instance, the company that lays off twenty thousand workers. That company thinks it was the right decision to save itself by cutting expenses and regrouping. Among those twenty thousand workers, some will think losing their job is devastating; others will think it's finally the freedom they've wanted to get away from that job. Some will think it gives them an opportunity to pursue something new while others will feel victimized and like they're left with no options. None of these thoughts is right or wrong; they are just thoughts, but if we examine what feelings each of those thoughts create, we can surely follow the path of action each thought will launch, and it won't be hard to predict the results each one will ultimately create.

<<< BONNIE'S STORY >>>

Bonnie was one of those twenty thousand laid-off workers. She was in her late fifties when she received her termination notice. She was devastated and terrified of the future. Bonnie was a divorced mother supporting two teens. She was a loyal employee who had planned to work at this company for life. She lived within her means and planned well for her future. She'd even bought her condo because it was close to work and checked all the boxes of security. Life seemed pretty certain. She enjoyed the social camaraderie at work with her colleagues, and when she was laid off, it was as if everything was "stolen" from her. She was a model employee that not only showed up for work and did her job well, but worked overtime willingly with a good attitude, demonstrating she was a team player.

When I first started coaching Bonnie, she spent numerous sessions talking about how unfair it was and how she felt robbed of her social connections. She was tired of feeling angry and bitter when she was typically such a happy person. Ironically, Bonnie thought she was angry and bitter because she was laid off, but what really caused her pain was her belief that what had happened was unfair and that she was being punished. Bonnie reacted to these thoughts by feeling angry and sad, but reacting isn't the same as processing feelings. As we worked together, Bonnie discovered she was well practiced at resisting feelings by stuffing them down because being angry or sad wasn't acceptable. Like many people, Bonnie was afraid that if she allowed her feelings to emerge, it would be like opening a faucet that couldn't be turned off. Ironically it's when we process and allow our feelings instead of resisting or reacting to them that they dissipate. When Bonnie learned to become the watcher of her feelings and to identify and allow the sensation of sadness to exist by noticing where it resided in her body, she felt the weight of sadness slowly dissipate. Anger and sadness could quickly reactivate but only when she focused on thinking she was a victim or that the situation was unfair and her life was ruined. She quickly learned it was her thoughts that activated her feelings.

Over time and a lot of tissue boxes, Bonnie was able to expand her awareness and consider what other thoughts were available even though her circumstances hadn't changed. She learned to ask herself new questions, which redirected her focus to a more resourceful place. For example, she asked, "How can I enjoy this free time?" Bonnie decided to use her saved-up air mileage to make a trip to visit both her twin brother and her best friend and reestablish the missing social connections she longed for. She also bravely followed up on a job lead that a friend gave her without limiting herself for all the reasons she thought she didn't qualify. She acted on it immediately whereas she previously would've sat in analysis paralysis. Bonnie interviewed and accepted that contract position, which paid her more money and offered more flexibility than ever. This caused her to do something radically different, which was to put her needs and desires first. She immediately gave notice to the short-term contract she had that was below her pay grade but paying the bills. She never would've had the confidence to put herself first and care about her outcome had she not learned to manage her thoughts and make decisions to please herself first.

* * * *

HOW TO MAKE THE "BEST" DECISION

There is one simple rule for making the best decision when you are choosing whether to leave something or to change a job, a relationship, or a place of residency: Get happy where you are, and then make the decision.

Of course, this seems completely counterintuitive and you are by now rolling your eyes and pointing out the obvious: "If I was happy in my job or relationship or in the place I was living, then why would I want to decide to leave?"

Again, I suggest asking a different question. Instead of asking, "Why do I want to leave?" ask "What am I looking for? What do I want?" When we focus on what we *don't* want, like the reasons we want to leave or discontinue a relationship, job, or place of residence, we keep those elements prominent in our minds. We attempt to control our universe and how we feel by changing the circumstances. That is actually backward. We do best if we change how we think and feel before we decide if and how to change the circumstances.

EXCEPTION RULE:

Your safety is of paramount concern. If you are in an abusive relationship that puts you (or your minor children) in physical or emotional peril, you must seek the legal and emotional support of professionals specifically trained to help with domestic abuse.

******Never stay in a situation that threatens or causes you harm.******

Get out first and explore later.

THOUGHT GEM

JUST DECIDE whatever decision you make is the ***best*** decision until you make the next one.

11 CHAPTER PREVENTING FUTURE REGRET

"Have more fear of regret than failure."

~ Thibaut ~

How do we create our future? We create our future *from our future beliefs* about what is possible. We don't create our future from our past. Our past is our past, and any regret about it is a poisonous waste of precious emotional and mental energy. Is it possible, then, to prevent future regret? One clue may come from the cautionary wisdom of those at the end of their lives. According to an Australian hospice worker, Bronnie Ware, who listened to and wrote about the stories of people on their deathbeds in her poignant book, *The Top Five Regrets of the Dying*, the most commonly occurring regret was the belief the person hadn't been true to themselves. They regretted not living an "authentic life" because they deferred their desires and decisions to satisfy the expectations of others.

Most people regretted the things they didn't do versus the things they did do, meaning they regretted the chances they never took, the places they never went, the things they never said, and the relationships they either didn't develop or the ones they let languish. Perhaps the most tragic of all regrets is the decision to not love oneself or appreciate one's inherent lovability and worthiness or, as noted, to "live a life true to myself, not the life others expected of me."

YOU CAN PREVENT FUTURE REGRET BY DECIDING IN ADVANCE THAT REGRET IS NOT AN OPTION.

Living your authentic life takes risk.

The following stories illustrate how Sharon and Layla took risks to lead the authentic lives that were calling to them.

SHARON'S STORY

I found myself turning fifty, living in the incredibly exciting New York City, in a fun, new marriage, and yet still waking up wanting to quit my job, throw my few prized possessions into a storage unit, and take off on a meandering cross-country road trip. I started buying travel books and marking the places I longed to visit and highlighting lists of all the off-the-beaten-path foodie spots I was going to track down to try. My husband and I spent hours looking at maps and dreaming up our vision of six months in motion.

There is no doubt that my decision to embrace my next adventure fully and enthusiastically was heavily influenced by the short life spans of both my mother and father and my commitment after their deaths to live fully and without the need for approval from others.

My mother's exceptional character and disposition as she faced a devastating diagnosis in her late forties informed my own teenage decisions and was an essential component that shifted the way I moved more freely through my own life.

My father's influence came in the form of open-minded acceptance and free thinking. Both were the necessary elements that ushered in a new way of thinking and a new way of being for me after I lost him in my twenties. My parents' unconditional love and role modeling gave me permission to pivot, move, try out new ideas, and even fail. It was all acceptable as I grew and changed.

As soon as I shared my husband's and my decision with family and friends, it became even more exciting and real for us, but it wasn't all easy. Many people needed to express their own fears and worries, and all the well-intentioned tales of catastrophe and doom weighed down my own natural optimism at times. But I would not be deterred. My inner wisdom was deeply committed to taking the leap of faith into the unknown.

What I did not know was that leaving my familiar world behind would open so many new, enriching, and wonderful possibilities and experiences for my life story. The road trip led to a move to Paris for six months, which led to a move to Napa Valley, California, and the beat goes on to this day.

* * * *

Sharon decided to quit her job and travel because she thought it was important to be free and fulfill her desires. Her parents' early deaths informed her decisions about heeding her inner wisdom and daring desire to live fully even in the absence of others' approval. There was no shortage of warnings and admonishments from well-meaning friends and family members about why she was making a bad decision, especially about giving up her apartment in New York City. In New York, people are loath to give up something as seemingly insignificant as a parking space because of the scarcity of good spots, let alone let go of an awesome apartment in a fabulous location. But Sharon decided she was up for the thrill and uncertainty of her adventure. She credits having a positive mindset as an intrinsic part of her nature that allowed her to hold her desire above the fears of others. She noted the decision was easier to make because she had a partner who was also on board for the adventure. Most importantly, she felt certain that no matter what happened during the journey, she could figure it out. It wasn't impulsive. The practicality of arranging the "hows" showed up organically and naturally as she thought ahead and envisioned what she would need to do to complete her living arrangement in New York and trade it in for plotting a course that still allowed plenty of room for spontaneity.

She answered each question as she planned the details of her journey, including: what furniture to save and store, what to give away, what to sell, what to discard; when to leave work; when to give notice on their apartment. She made more decisions about whether to give up or defer new projects as well as how to create a stealthy work-from-the-road opportunity (before remote work was a thing!). Finally, Sharon and her husband purchased a comfier, bigger vehicle that would suit them for the long days of driving.

Were there any setbacks? Sharon shared another story.

The worst setback was on our very first night; we drove south three hours to Delaware to make our initial stop. It was a very cold January evening, and we were both exhausted from the final push of closing up our apartment and leaving town. We were so tired that we forgot to bring into the house our one case of special wines that we had saved and carefully chosen to bring on the trip. These were wines from many of our travels to Europe or Napa Valley that we had saved for a "special occasion." All the wine froze overnight, and eleven out of twelve bottles were ruined. Otherwise, the trip was quite magical. Two months into the journey we had already started planning the following six months in Paris!

* * * *

LAYLA'S STORY

As a native Floridian, living in Asheville, North Carolina, I felt like a fish out of water, a landlocked mermaid who was dying to get back to her home state. I had come to Asheville with my then husband and two young children because of a business deal my husband created. We had a very traditional marriage, and I always viewed being a stay-at-home mom as a privilege to influence and impact the lives of my children. It was the best way I knew I could instill my values and morals. Because I chose not to have an outside career, it allowed me to be involved with the children's school and enrichment activities, as well as to engage in charitable organizations and attend and lead Bible studies. My husband was the family breadwinner. On the surface we had an idyllic marriage with each of us choosing the roles we wanted most, but there were many dark shadows and secrets, especially surrounding my husband's business.

One day, without notice, my husband simply vanished from our lives. The last thing he did before fleeing the country was empty our bank accounts and lock me out of accessing any funds. I suddenly had no income, no savings, and no backup plan. As a single mom I decided the most important thing I could do was provide stability for my two children. Although I was eager to leave Asheville, I decided to stay for the next twelve years while my kids were in school so they could stay with their friends and regain a sense of certainty. Little by little I sold the contents of our home to keep money coming in and the bill collectors away.

What would I do with the next twelve years of my life? Instead of waiting "until they grew up," I decided to live into the possibility of my plans right now. At fifty, I decided to pursue my interest in nutrition and become a certified wellness coach. Since I'd also practiced yoga for decades, I began offering "Flourish Retreats" at my home, which combined doing what I loved most: teaching yoga and teaching how to cook nutritious and delicious foods. These were so fun and successful that I began dreaming about what else was possible. This led me to boldly apply to Lululemon and be hired as their "oldest" yoga instructor. Fast-forward a decade and finally my kids were grown. The day of "UNTIL" actually arrived! The decision to fulfill my long-term dream of returning to Florida and starting a new life bubbled with possibility.

I had this grand idea to rent a waterfront house with a pool for the season in Palm Beach and host a weeklong destination wellness retreat at the house. I then discovered I could apply for a "Lululemon seasonal transfer" to Palm Beach. While I knew it would be costly, I wanted it so badly and knew I had to follow my heart. I was ready!

Lululemon's corporate culture is all about goal setting and becoming the best version of yourself. One of their manifestos that resonated with me was "Live in possibility!" It triggered something in me and made me ask myself some hard questions about the decision I wanted to make yet feared. It made me ask myself, "What is the worst thing that could happen about this decision?" Well, lots of doubt and limiting questions surfaced. "What if I spend all my money renting the house? What if I invite people and nobody shows up for my retreat?" But living in possibility meant believing that it just might work out, that this dream I had was possible! In order to make it happen, I had to get uncomfortable. I had to put myself out there and hope people would come.

One of my greatest fears is failure, but I've come to realize that if I fail to take a risk because I'm afraid I might not succeed, I'm just really living small, and I don't believe we were put on this earth to live small. I believe we are here to live abundant lives full of richness and adventure.

"Do one thing every day that scares you" is another Lululemon manifesto, so I decided to embrace my fear and willingness to take risks if it meant I might get my outcome. I rented a house and hosted a beautiful weeklong wellness retreat in Palm Beach for the season. Four people came. It ended up being a huge success, we had the time of our lives, and it paid for my month of rent at the house.

That decision prompted my next best decision, which was to move permanently to Florida. A bonus was that both of my children moved here too. I couldn't be happier, and I'm so grateful for the courage I mustered up to follow my dreams. Not one regret!

* * * *

Layla didn't entertain past regrets about her "failed" marriage, with all its legal and financial complications, as a reason to limit her future. If anything, she decided that circumstance created an opportunity for a new vision that was deeply compelling. Layla's story illustrates how she regret-proofed her life by living into her future possibilities. It's true she risked spending money on a rental that might have resulted in no one showing up, but she chose to think of that money as an investment in herself and her dream. She was so decisive and committed, she regret-proofed herself by acting passionately toward her outcome. So often we stop ourselves from doing something as a means of protecting ourselves from failure, but the irony is we *pre-fail* by never giving ourselves the opportunity to attempt what we desire. Not only do we suffer by never getting to experience our desire, but we add to the suffering by convincing ourselves we are powerless, not resilient, and can't take risks. Layla didn't expect her children to come to Florida and didn't influence their decisions, but welcomed them as an added bonus. Her business continues to thrive, and more importantly she has learned to trust herself, take risks, and have her own back while she continues to create value in the retreats she provides.

THOUGHT GEM

JUST DECIDE regret is not an option. Trust yourself to take a risk and lead the authentic life you know is calling.

PAUSE AND REFLECT

1. What's one thing you will do to regret-proof your life? When will you do it? (Deciding on a date and a time makes it real and is critical to achieving the result.)

2. Why is it important?

3. Why might you regret *not* making this decision? What would it cost you emotionally, financially, or health-wise?

12

CHAPTER

MINING THE GOLD OF "FAILED & FABULOUS" DECISIONS

"You may be disappointed if you fail, but you are doomed if you don't try."

~ Beverly Sills ~

What does it mean to mine the gold of failed decisions? I like to think of it as sifting through the rubble of a perceived failure to find the golden nuggets of learning. This is an exercise I do with my clients in which we evaluate with some perspective and distance the results of a previously made decision. If we start the "mining" too soon, our judgment may be clouded by our immediate feelings of doubt, which are caused by our thoughts.

WHAT DOES FAILURE MEAN?

Dictionary definition: *The omission of expected or required action.*

However, I feel that there are two kinds of failure: failing *in advance* by never getting started and failing to meet the expected or required action to achieve your desired outcome.

Let's talk about failing in advance first. How often have we left decisions and actions languishing in the pool of "I'll do it someday"? We reason that we're scared, we don't know how, we're afraid of failing, yet we cut to the chase and actually fail in advance. The very thing we fear, we willingly walk into. Failing in advance gnaws at our self-esteem. We think it keeps us safe, but in reality it's uncomfortable, and it keeps us stuck—or worse, provides evidence that we are failures.

The second type of failure is actually doing the thing and not having it work out. Maybe we ask for a raise, attempt to launch a business, decide to lose weight, go on a dating site, or try an experimental treatment to improve our health. When the actions we take don't yield the results we want, we have to get curious and reevaluate. If we are truly committed to the goal we are attempting to achieve, resigning after a few "failed" attempts stops us from ever getting what we want. What if we viewed failing as *feedback*—not as a signal to stop, but to learn? What if failing was synonymous with learning?

This is not just a matter of semantics. Learning means that failing is part of the process of making your future decision(s). Think like a scientist: We have a hypothesis. We test it. We evaluate the outcome. The hypothesis either created the result we intended or it didn't. It's from this scientific vantage point that we can examine our decisions and extract the gold, the lessons learned, the new ideas and intentions that result from identifying what we didn't desire as an outcome. All too often we think failure is a signal to give up. We blame people and circumstances, and we relinquish the power we have. We often end up feeling victimized or like we're living at the effect of our circumstances. Whenever we are at the effect of our circumstances, we are at a dead end. Yes, things can and do happen to us. We can be stopped at a red light when someone rear-ends us, but we still have agency and power over what happens next.

It's important to mine the gold of fabulous decisions as well as failed ones since there will be information and strategies you want to replicate. In the same way we avoid things that didn't bring us toward our desired outcome, we want to replicate the things that did!

Hypothesize, test, evaluate.

A "MINING" EXAMPLE

Marie came to me with a complaint about her abusive boss. She felt powerless about the unfair expectations he had of her. She was so upset that she quit her job. In our work together Marie was able to use the techniques presented in Chapter 8 to separate the facts from the story and recognize where her true power lay. Let's see what she gained from our coaching session.

Marie started by telling me her boss was "abusive." I asked what that meant to her. She told me, "He demands that I do things I've never learned or been trained to do and then criticizes me when I get it wrong, even though he's never trained me."

"Let's dive into this example," I told her. "Of course, let's do so by starting with the facts and not the story."

It becomes easier to get clarity and mine the gold of past "failures" if we simplify the circumstances, so I asked her to focus on one event that perhaps was her worst or most recent defeat. If the boss said words she remembered, I told her to write those words down.

"Now as you think about the words the boss said," I asked, "what did you make them mean? Maybe the boss said, 'You screwed up this contract.' What was your thought at that moment? Was it 'I haven't been trained to write contracts'? Now ask yourself how you felt at that moment. Did you feel powerless? Make sure to stay in that moment and that event."

Next I encouraged her to consider the actions she took. A good way to observe those past actions is to imagine someone following you with a video camera. What would they capture you doing or not doing if you were feeling powerless because you were thinking, "I'm not trained to do this"? I encouraged her to list all the things she did or didn't do. "Actions could also include what you didn't say aloud," I said, "but that you said in your mind in that spinning, ruminating way." For example, she might have thought, "I wrote the contract as best I could. I delayed writing the contract till the last minute but made sure to submit it on time. I didn't ask for help. I didn't ask questions. I kept telling myself I didn't know what I was doing."

Eventually the result Marie created was that she missed the opportunity to learn how to properly write a contract. Though she thought the reason she felt powerless was because her boss said, "You screwed up the contract," the real reason she felt powerless was *her own limiting thought:* "I'm not trained to write contracts."

Do you notice the person really responsible for knowing how to write the contract is Marie? This is where mining the gold of failed decisions becomes a powerful learning tool.

Some people would argue it's the boss's job to train or teach their subordinates, and while that may be true, if that teaching is not forthcoming and Marie wanted to do her job well, what else could she have thought?

Someone might say, "She could've asked her boss or coworker." That is a valuable action to take, but it would not be a logical action to take from the limiting thought, "My boss should teach me what to do." Do you see how there is no power in that thought? You can't control your boss—or anyone else for that matter. There might be many different thoughts that would have put Marie in a powerful versus a powerless state of emotion. Remember, our thoughts are just sentences in our heads. A few different thoughts, such as, "I'm resourceful. I solve problems. I ask important questions and get answers so I can do my job well," would create a feeling of determination that would have resulted in very different actions. Marie might have still gotten the contract wrong, but once you blame someone else for what you are *not* doing, you can never get the results you desire. Leaving an "abusive" job (i.e., changing the circumstances) without changing your thoughts will only lead to the next abusive, toxic job situation. Consider what you want instead. Will seeking a boss that encourages questions be something you'll put on your list?

Whether you've left a job like Marie or made some other decision you regret, reflecting on this past "failure" can help you analyze any missteps and prevent them in future. Just remember to zero in on one specific example, mine it for your feelings and thoughts in that moment, and identify any limiting thoughts or other negative choices that could be remedied the next time a similar situation crops up. You are not your "failures." They are part of your life, but you can choose to use them as the crossbar to help you vault successfully over your next decision.

THOUGHT GEM

JUST DECIDE that the word "failure" is synonymous with feedback and learning. Let failure be a measure of success for the risks you are taking.

Sometimes we haven't even engaged in a decision that is a failure, but because of external pressures, like the way we see successful people living their lives, we feel that it is one. Take hope from the positive spin Dyana put on her version of this story.

DYANA'S STORY

"What's my purpose? What is my passion? Why am I here? What is the meaning of all of this?" These questions have been asked since the dawn of humankind and were the same questions that had been plaguing me for much of my adulthood. There I was, in my late forties, looking back at my life and the work I had done—junior manufacturing engineer, chocolatier, X-ray technician, help desk at an aerospace company, quality assurance tester for an educational software developer—all leading up to the most complex job of all, at-home parent of two. While raising my kids, all thanks to a loving and supportive spouse, I also was able to pursue certificate and diploma classes in massage therapy, video production, and grant writing.

However, in reviewing my life, I was becoming more and more despondent. People my age appeared to have determined their glorious purpose, found that one guiding principle, that tower of flame in their soul, and were thriving in their chosen professions, solidly walking the career path in front of them (and making good money at it!).

What have I done with my life? In my depressed state, constantly asking myself the question, "What is my purpose?" was causing me stress and anxiety. Over time, this question gradually became shadowed by another more ominous one, "If I can't find my true passion and purpose in my life, would my family, friends, the world, be OK—or even better off—without me?" Society and all the self-help books I'd read told me I was supposed to have discovered what I was born to do by now, but I hadn't. I seemed to be a "Jill of All Trades" and yet a master of none. I felt lost, confused, and directionless. I felt like a failure.

Perhaps life saw the dark turn my years of questioning about purpose and passion had taken and took mercy on me in 2015. I happened to be on the internet, and the Universe placed Elizabeth Gilbert's Super Soul Sessions speech, "The Flight of the Hummingbird: The Curiosity-Driven Life," in my search results and changed my life.

In her presentation, Gilbert explained that she had come to know that the world was made up of two types of people: jackhammers and hummingbirds. Gilbert herself identifies as a jackhammer, which she defines as someone who becomes consumed by one singular passion: "We don't look up and we don't veer, and we're just focused on that until the end of time. It's efficient, you get a lot done," she admits, "but we tend to be obsessive and fundamentalist and sometimes a little difficult and loud." Hummingbirds, on the other hand, "move from flower to flower, from field to field, trying this, trying that, and two things happen. They create incredibly rich, complex lives for themselves, and they also end up pollinating the world." A hummingbird person's service to humanity is fulfilled by "bringing an idea from here to over here where you learn something else… so that your perspective ends up keeping the entire culture aerated and mixed up and open to the new and fresh."

Tears of relief and joy streamed down my face by the end of the twenty-nine-minute video! As if a switch had been miraculously flipped, my thoughts about myself and the path my life had taken were forever changed. I let go of all the pressure I was making the word "passion" mean, and instead I decided to do something much simpler: follow my curiosity. I decided to trade in the anxiety of chasing an elusive passion that I've always felt pressured to find and allow myself the freedom to trust and curiously explore my many varied interests.

Since embracing my hummingbird nature, I've allowed myself to continue to pursue my interests in literacy tutoring, culinary arts, and, most recently, a career as a pharmacy technician. Yes, my CV may look like a patchwork coat of many colors, but now, instead of feeling embarrassed, I'm proud of it! I've been able to bring wisdom from lessons learned at each stop along my journey to each successive environment I find myself in.

* * * *

Dyanna's circumstances didn't change at all. Her problem didn't stem from having a variety of jobs on her resume. It was her *thought* that she wasn't finding her passion that caused her to feel deep inadequacy and suffering. When she *thought* about herself in this new, empowering way of "pollinating the world with fresh ideas," her entire life shifted to self-appreciation and fulfillment. This reframing technique is how she mined the gold of her fabulous decisions.

PAUSE AND REFLECT:

What are the three worst decisions you've made? Give three examples of past "failures."

1. ______________________________

2. ______________________________

3. ______________________________

For each situation, write down what you made the decision(s) surrounding that failure mean.

- Why did you decide it was a bad or wrong decision?

____

____

____

____

- Did any surprising benefits or by-products occur because of your decision?

____

____

____

____

If you had to rewrite the story (without changing the circumstances), what gold would you find? What would the title of your new story be? For instance, "How I Got Divorced and Didn't Get What I Wanted" might be retitled "How I Got Divorced and Created What I Really Wanted."

When we have past failures, or the sense of a past failure, we don't have to let it drag us down. Instead, we can analyze a specific moment we have considered a failure for lessons we can take into the future with us, or we can reframe our thinking about a particular story we tell about ourselves so that it has a more positive feel. Both actions help us, in their own ways, feel empowered to make future decisions with confidence.

Looking ahead, we will use the final section of this book to tie this lesson in with all the others you've learned over the course of JUST DECIDE and to offer up some practical guidance to help you strengthen those decision-making muscles.

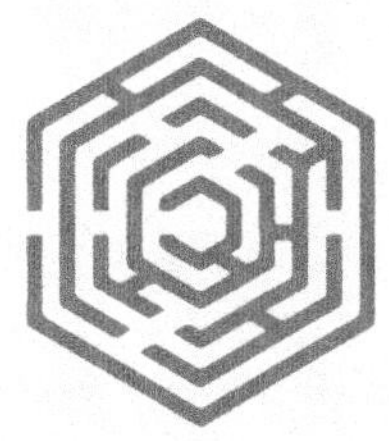

SECTION IV

PUTTING IT ALL TOGETHER

This section takes decision-making to the next level using your whole brain, not just your analytical reasoning. We'll close out the book with these next few chapters by introducing you to the secret sauce of intuition, then applying it along with other strategies for making more complex decisions. Finally, you'll learn how to use obstacles as indicators that help you decide what your next steps in any given situation should be.

13 CHAPTER THE SECRET SAUCE OF INTUITION

"Trust your instincts. Intuition doesn't lie."

~ Oprah Winfrey ~

Beyond rational, analytic thinking is a superpower we all possess, but we may not give it its just attention or appreciation: *intuition*. What exactly is intuition? According to the Oxford English Dictionary, intuition is "the ability to understand or know something immediately, without conscious reasoning." We commonly refer to an experience of intuition as a "gut feeling" that either alerts us to something not quite right, perhaps even terribly wrong, or energetically drives us to make a decision with such pristine clarity and wisdom that it feels divinely inspired.

As it turns out, calling intuition a "gut feeling" is biologically accurate. Neuroscientists confirm that our gut and the emotional limbic part of our brains are connected by millions of neurons. Sometimes we get a visceral feeling in our gut, but intuition can present itself in other sensory ways or be felt in other bodily organs; that is, it may show up in things we see, hear, or feel. We may have an instantaneous vision. We may hear a literal voice outside of ourselves calling us or stating something emphatically, we may feel a sensation in our hearts or at the back of our necks, or we may have an all-over goose bump experience.

This begs the question: Can intuition be mapped in the brain? Yes, according to a team of researchers at the University of Iowa, who discovered that the brain's so-called "axis of intuition" is located in the ventromedial prefrontal cortex (vmPFC), which happens to be smack in the middle of our foreheads. Eastern religions and ancient yogis have long referred to this area as the third eye, well before there were any MRI machines.

The third eye is the place where we "see" that which is not physical. We commonly know this as our sixth sense, and it corresponds to the sixth chakra or energy point in our bodies. In Sanskrit, it is known as "the seat of intuition." This invisible yet powerful third eye functions as a person's center of wisdom, conscience, and higher consciousness.

Some of the most powerful, creative, and financially savvy leaders understand and apply the leverage of intuition. Steve Jobs referred to intuition as "more powerful than intellect." Jeff Bezos, founder and executive chairman of Amazon, said, "All of my best decisions in business and in life have been made with heart, intuition, guts—not [with] analysis." When Oprah Winfrey was interviewed about "what she knew for sure," she spoke about trusting her intuition, stating, "Learning to trust your instincts, using your intuitive sense of what's best for you, is paramount for any lasting success. I've trusted the still, small voice of intuition my entire life. And the only time I've made mistakes is when I didn't listen."

For our purposes we are going to discuss intuition as that extra-special sauce that guides you in decision-making beyond the rational data collection of our analytic brain. The good news is we don't have to choose between reasoning or intuition to make decisions; we can deliberately and powerfully include both.

The best way to cultivate your intuitive powers is first to acknowledge they exist.

In her carefully detailed book that's full of rich stories, *Your Essential Whisper: Six Ways to Recognize, Trust, and Follow Inner Guidance With Absolute Certainty*, La Rue Eppler describes and differentiates among the six distinct experiences that help you identify your "Whisper" or "voice of inner guidance." She specifies, "The voice of the Whisper is undeniable and totally different from the mind chatter or stream of our incessant thoughts. These distinctive qualities are revealed as specific sensations and inner feelings of peace, sureness, energy, and joy."

Eppler shares four strategies to heighten your ability to access your inner guidance and open your awareness. These include: conscious choice, focused attention, focused intention, and noticing. Eppler's book offers interactive exercises to help you recognize and cultivate your intuitive powers.

You can start listening to your intuitive voice by simply committing to a regular practice of meditation involving sitting, breathing, and focusing your attention. If you are about to dismiss meditation as impossible to do because your mind is "busy and you just can't focus," welcome to the world of humans! The secret of meditation is not to resist the myriad of thoughts clamoring for your attention, but in fact to notice them and let them go. You will do it thousands of times before you get a nanosecond of that blissful inner voice, but considering the bountiful payoff meditation delivers, it's worthy of at least your curiosity and commitment to practice for a period of time.

PAUSE AND REFLECT

1. Recall a time where your intuition led you to make an empowered decision even if others tried to dissuade you.

____

____

____

2. Did your intuition appear as a vision or through a dream, a voice, or a feeling?

____

____

____

3. How did you know it was the right decision? What did you feel?

____

____

4. How will you cultivate your intuitive skills to guide you further?

____

____

THOUGHT GEM

JUST DECIDE that your superpowers of decision involve both your intuitive sensibilities and your analytic reasoning skills.

CHAPTER 14 AS SOON AS YOU DECIDE, PREPARE TO BE CHALLENGED

"Learn to find your 'do' in doubt."

~ Tsgoyna Tanzman ~

It's going to take courage and decisiveness to make a decision and declare it out loud. For that brief moment of elation you will feel certain and determined. You might even feel invincible and have such clarity that it will almost certainly be a high. A weight has been lifted; you are intentional and deliberate and determined. Then you tell someone, your best friend, your sister, your mother, your child, or your partner. In that split second of confession, you may be met with doubt, dissuasion, criticism, dismissiveness, resistance, and flat-out refusal to agree with or support you. Suddenly what you thought was so clear and perfect has dissolved into a pool of doubt and instability. The risk here is that you are going to be influenced, if not convinced, by all the naysayers. This will be another deciding moment. Will you follow your guidance, stand behind your well-thought-out decision, or relent and retreat? If you do retreat, will you like your reasons for doing so?

Too often there is a belief that a decision is all-or-nothing—it can only be my decision or someone else's—but that just isn't true. There are factors like timing, frequency, and intensity that modulate a decision. You could, for example, decide to leave a job, but the timing and all that is involved in leaving can be moderated. The same goes for divorce and the way it will play out. It's important nonetheless to consider what the decision is and, most importantly, your reason for the decision.

You are going to have to have a very meaningful and purposeful "why" to hold firm to your decision. Do you like your reasons? It's not that you'll need to justify your reasons to anyone but yourself, but recall from this book's introduction that the word "decide" comes from the Latin literally for "to cut off." Once you decide, the challenge for you will be to feel firm in your decision and take the next logical step toward that new thought.

It's going to be uncomfortable; you can pretty much expect that. Whenever we break out of a familiar pattern and show up differently to those people who expect us to be a certain way, everyone is shaken. That shift is often jarring to those who know us and expect certain reactions and behaviors from us. If you are not challenged by someone else, you will likely be challenged by your own doubts and fears. They may or may not show up immediately; they may hang back and wait, giving you the sense you are invincible. But in the event those doubts show up at the start or slip in while you are well underway, know that the turbulence is part of the deal. Any time you are creating something new or stepping into an unknown area there will be, according to Elizabeth GIlbert, the author of *Big Magic,* the necessary "shit sandwiches" to eat along the way. Gilbert is referring to the parts of the process of creativity that aren't fun or convenient, but that need to happen to get the job done.

It's important to remember that doubts are just thoughts. They are sentences in your mind, and you could probably counter each one of your doubts with another thought that may or may not make you feel better.

While this book focuses on you as the only person who can make your decisions, consulting with trustworthy sources to gather information, especially regarding medical, legal, financial, or spiritual decisions, is highly recommended. Trust yourself to know the difference between when you might be resistant to input because a part of you may agree with another's concern versus the ability to objectively listen to another and make a decision from your best place of knowing.

We often try to defend ourselves by trying to convince others why our decision is reasonable, logical, and how it could also benefit them. In our effort to be persuasive by trying to control another's feelings, we actually widen the gap of agreement. Your work is changing your own mind and being in agreement with it. Stay in your own lane.

PAUSE AND REFLECT

Now is the time to root out those wiley, life-sucking self-doubts and make a plan for how you'll handle them before you even announce your decision.

Use these *workbook* exercises to anticipate what obstacles might show up that would cause you to feel less confident in your decision.

1. What will you have to think to shore up your feelings of decisiveness and certainty in the face of opposition?

____

____

____

____

2. What will you do or not do if your decision is questioned by others?

____

____

____

____

3. What can you expect as your own obstacles of self-doubt, fear, and so on?

____

____

____

Make sure to empty your mind of *all* obstacles by writing them down. Once the obstacles are out of your head and you can observe them, they can become the blueprint for knowing what steps you will have to take to stand firm in your decision or goal, no matter what.

THOUGHT GEM

JUST DECIDE first and foremost to have your own back. Your opinion matters. Make sure you have agreement with yourself first, and the rest will follow.

15 CHAPTER "JUST DECIDE" STRATEGIES

"You are only one decision away from a totally different life."

~ Anonymous ~

At last, the "how to" section, full of JUST DECIDE strategies! These strategies should work in tandem with other practical suggestions you've received throughout the book. Caution, though: If you've jumped to this section because you are so eager to JUST DECIDE, in skipping out on the rest of the book, you will have missed the most important part of the transformation. Becoming aware of your thoughts and feelings about any decision or circumstance is critical to the process *before* you take action.

If this is you, no need to feel guilty! Once you have read the rest of the book, bookmark this page and refer to it frequently to gain practice and familiarity with the process.

We are going to drill down into the hows of evaluating a decision (e.g., risks, benefits, obstacles) soon, but for now, you have to first decide what you want.

WHEN YOU DON'T KNOW WHERE TO START... START WITH THE END IN MIND

The best practice for making a decision is to begin with the end in mind, to start by determining what you want the result of your decision to be. This is a time-trusted strategy from the ancient and wisest Indian gurus to the modern-day writer Stephen Covey in his book, *The 7 Habits of Highly Effective People.*

I hear you, friend. Maybe you're frustrated and saying, "I don't know what I want! That's the problem."

Maybe you're confused as to whether to stay married or get divorced. Maybe you're conflicted about switching jobs. Whatever your decision, if you know where you want to go and most importantly why you want to get there, you can connect the dots in reverse to make a plan using careful strategies.

Use the workbook pages to start exploring. Usually we are better at identifying what we don't want because what we don't want is our pain point. It's the thing we are trying to avoid. I don't want a boss who yells. I don't want a partner who cheats on me. I don't want a nine-to-five job. The thing is our brains don't really process the negative word (i.e., "don't") any more than your GPS could interpret where you don't want to go. Imagine what would happen if you tried to program your GPS but said, "Well, I don't want to go to the airport, I don't want to go to the library, and I don't want to go to the hospital." You'd never get out of the parking lot! This activity of declaring what we don't want, however, gives us the springboard for deciding what we do want. We can shift from, for instance, "I don't want a boss who is irrational and micromanages" to "I want to manage myself and have a boss who wants her employees to be self-regulated and accountable."

Once you've created a want list, let's look at the *why* behind it. The why is so important because it is what will pull you through the very challenging and uncomfortable passages of getting from where you are to where you want to be. Doing something new will almost always be uncomfortable, but you will be trading short-term discomfort for long-term sustainable fulfillment and expansion.

Why do you want the thing you want? Is it to relieve pain? Is it to grow? Is it out of a need for protection or a deeper self-love for expansion? What do you think you will feel as a result of having this goal? As you've already learned, the only reason why we want anything is because of how we think we will feel in the attainment of it. This question will be explored more deeply toward the end of this chapter, when we look at five practical strategies, specifically Strategy 4: "Activate the Feeling State."

As you start with the end in mind as your first strategy in fail-proof decision-making, you set your guidance system to know where and why you want to get there. You don't have to focus on the how yet. The "hows" are the action steps you will take to get there, but you must first know where it is you want to go. The where does not necessarily refer to an actual place, but rather to a metaphorical state of being. Do you want to be married or single? Do you want to begin or end a job, make an investment, begin schooling or a course of study? Do you want to begin a new physical endeavor, sport, or body transformation; write a book; build a house; travel the world; become a speaker, filmmaker, or political advocate? Do you want to terminate or resolve a relationship with a child, friend, relative, boss, or partner?

As you begin with the end in mind, you must assume what it would be like if you knew you couldn't fail. This mindset is important because it's the only thing that will give you the courage to get out of the cave. Is it likely you will encounter some rough roads ahead? Yes, but the mindset that knows why it's committed to the outcome—and what outcome it expects—will be able to tolerate and process the bumps and detours along the way.

FIVE PRACTICAL STRATEGIES FOR REACHING YOUR DECISION

Along with the best practice of beginning with the end in mind, there are five key strategies I use each time I make a conscious, empowered decision. These five strategies are to be used together, first quieting your mind and grounding you in your why, before moving on to a sense of positivity toward your decision as you declare it and move forward to taking action.

STRATEGY 1: QUIET YOUR MIND

Why You Do This:

Taking five minutes to reach a place of centeredness, awareness, and neutrality will allow you to make decisions with greater clarity and alignment. It's important to *create feelings from the future to call yourself to the future.*

How You Do This:

- Start by focusing on your breath. Become aware of your inhalations and exhalations without forcing them. Notice how, as you sit and empty your mind, your breathing slows and self-regulates. Resist judging your busy mind and its many thoughts. Just allow those thoughts to pass as if you were watching clouds pass slowly by you.
- Practice "coming to your senses" by focusing on one thing each of your senses is experiencing: the subtle taste in your mouth or its sense of moistness; the most distant and faintest sound you hear (e.g., the vibration of an electrical device); the lights or images you see behind your closed eyelids; the spark of energy you feel when your fingertips touch; and the most minute smell that you can discern. Allow this soft, slow focus to become fully present.
- Some people may find it easier to focus on an animal, a place, or a person they love that allows them to release good feelings.
- Repeat this phrase: "I ask for guidance" or "I'm open to receiving guidance." Don't force anything. Notice if you become frustrated because you are thinking, "Nothing is happening." Simply notice that thought without judgment. Rather, tune into the sensation of frustration. Be an observer and notice how and what that vibration of frustration feels like in your body. As you mentally narrate the shape, intensity, color, and descriptive sensation of the vibration, you will likely see it dissipate.
- Your only purpose at this stage is to be present and plant the intention:
  "I allow access to my inner guide."

STRATEGY 2: NAME YOUR DECISION AND WHY YOU WANT IT

Why You Do This:

When making a decision, you are preparing yourself to cut off other choices so you can singularly focus on moving in the direction of your desire. Once you make your decision, you create a goal, and your "why" will be what calls you to achieve your outcome regardless of the difficult transitions. Just because you align with a decision doesn't mean you're not going to have some rocky roads along the way.

How You Do This:

Answer these questions:

What is the decision I want to make?

____

____

Why do I want to make this decision?
(List your reasons for doing so.)

____

____

When do I need to make a choice?

____

____

STRATEGY 3: WRITE IT DOWN

Why You Do This:

It's important to get what's in your head out of it: your decision, your fears about it, how you might reach it, and so on. When you see your written words, you can evaluate your thoughts from a more objective place instead of trying to make sense of a jumble of circulating thoughts inside your head. We can then create organization and clarity.

How You Do This:

Use a blank piece of paper and pencil or the downloadable worksheets to write down everything you're thinking and feeling about your decision, good and bad. Get all your thoughts on paper, then look at them. Were you harboring good pieces of advice toward tackling your problem that you didn't know you had? What self-limiting or judgmental thoughts will you need to look out for as you stay committed to your decision?

STRATEGY 4: ACTIVATE THE FEELING STATE

Why You Do This:

Our feelings create our actions, so we want to be in the best feeling state to make the most informed decision. Your brain circuitry retains feeling states (good and bad and everything in between); that's why you can have an instant physical response to a person, smell, song, taste, or event long after it has happened. If you notice your thoughts drifting to the past, take that energy and refocus on your future. Focus on feeling good because you've activated good feelings.

> **Please note**
>
> You are practicing feeling good on purpose. You are simply activating a resourceful state. These feelings are unrelated to the decision you are about to make.

How You Do This:

- Call to mind a good feeling.
- Notice where in your body you feel this good feeling.
- Mentally describe the feeling. Is it light? Bubbly? Warm? Calming? Does it move and radiate?
- Begin to imagine that you have a dial (like the kind on a radio) that you can turn to amplify the good feelings and radiate them to all parts of your body.
- Imagine this good feeling within your body and in a field around you, creating a cocoon of light, love, and safety.

- Let this feeling amplify. At its peak, touch your pinky to your thumb to create your *resource anchor* (refer back to Chapter 9, "Do You Want What You Have?" for guidance). Maintain the connection just until the intensity starts to wane and then release your fingers. This resource anchor is like a power-up tool. You've programmed your neurology to activate this state by touching your fingers and quickly retriggering your resourceful state. It will take practice to build this association, but just like a certain smell or song can instantaneously return you to a feeling of the past, so can this brain hack.

STRATEGY 5: DECLARE YOUR DECISION AND MOVE FORWARD

Why You Do This:

Making a decision moves you forward. (Remember the car analogy; this is the gas pedal moment to take action.) Only from this conscious feeling state, even if it's one of discomfort, do you take action. Stalling out at this moment will prevent any learning or forward movement. Once you make a decision and begin taking action, the "hows" of what you have to do will become apparent. Immediately as you make the decision, fears, doubts, and "blocks" will surface. You may initially feel terrible, but remember that nothing's gone wrong. This is a signal that you are growing, and those blocks will become the stepping stones for achieving your outcome.

How You Do This:

Complete and use this fill-in phrase:

I've decided to ________________, and I feel ________________.

Even if I feel ______________________, I am committed to ________________. I trust myself to figure it out, no matter what future challenges come. I've got my back. I know that deciding is what launches me into the life I am designing and choosing on purpose.

Only I truly know what's best for my life. I am excited, curious, and willing to embrace it all.

These five strategies may seem like a lot of steps to take before you can make a decision, but the more you practice them, the more automatic they'll become until they are your default setting. When this happens, they'll come to take no time at all, and you will face each decision laid before you with confidence, an abundance mindset, and joy.

CHAPTER 16 THE BEAUTY OF NEVER GETTING IT DONE

"Don't go through life; grow through life."

~ Eric Butterworth ~

Here's a news flash: As long as you're alive, you will always have decisions to make. The more decisions you make in your life, the more confident you will become in making others. In this chapter, we'll close out by reviewing some of the key concepts related to how our thoughts create our feelings and ultimately show us our results. We'll challenge the concept "It's too late" by sharing the stories of women who continue to be examples of what's possible in their later years. Finally, you'll be prompted to explore what is possible for you.

Goal setting does not expire at age fifty or sixty or even one hundred. Goals are about being, having, and doing what you want as you create and expand your life. And you already know that every goal begins with a decision. Let's see how Aileen focused on the future to make her decisions.

AILEEN'S STORY

In my forties I faced three life-changing decisions at once: Should I start a small business with a partner? Should I accept a six-figure job offer from a promising biopharma company? Should I enroll in an MBA program? I only had two weeks to decide.

Up till that point in my life, I'd never questioned my purpose or calling. I was a good employee who knew how to work a nine-to-five job. I didn't know about inner guidance. I didn't know that my soul was searching for growth and new experiences. But when the book 10-10-10 *by Suzy Welch serendipitously fell into my lap, I began to examine my thoughts. The essence of the book was to ask three simple questions when making difficult decisions: What are the consequences of my decision in ten minutes? In ten months? In ten years?*

Feeling curious, I applied it to my situation.

1. Should I start my own business?

In ten minutes: I'll have doubt and confusion, as I haven't worked with a lawyer, CPA, or bank and because I still need a logo, web design, funding, and so on.

In ten months: The business will be demanding, and I may have more doubts and uncertainty.

In ten years: No matter what the outcome of my business, I'll be proud of myself for stepping out of my comfort zone and fulfilling my dream. Even if I fail, I can still find an employer, but I'll work with an appreciation for my employer's success. So yes to the business!

2. Should I accept the job offer?

In ten minutes: I'll be happy with a steady paycheck.

In ten months: I may complain about commuting, traveling, and time away from my children.

In ten years: I'll likely continue the path as an employee, perhaps in another job. I'd feel that I lived one year ten times. No to the job!

3. Should I get an MBA degree?

In ten minutes: I'll be happy, as I have always wanted to study business administration, recharge my battery, and learn new skills.

In ten months: I'll have pain—studying after work, writing essays, and paying tuition.

In ten years: I'll be proud of myself. I'll show my children that self-motivated learning is fun and fulfilling and you are never too old to go to school. Yes to MBA!

Eight years later, I'm proud to say that my business is thriving and I achieved that MBA. Do I still have doubts from time to time? Of course! As long as I am growing, I will have doubts and challenges to overcome. An unexpected area of growth came as a result of my MBA program: I discovered a love of writing. This propelled me to write an Amazon #1 bestselling book, Habits for Better Vision: 20 Scientifically Proven Ways to Improve Your Eyesight Naturally.

* * * *

Aileen used a unique decision-making strategy in which she futurized her thoughts, feelings, and actions to determine her results ahead of time. This future focus enabled her to try on the thoughts and feelings she projected she'd experience and to determine what would be the best choice. Could she anticipate every obstacle? Of course not, but as obstacles or problems appeared, so did the seeds of solution. One interesting side note is that we don't have to wait until we accomplish the thing before we feel proud or fulfilled. If we choose those feelings to accompany us along the journey, they will be the "power-ups" that continue to fuel us on our way. Remember the strategy of "I'll feel proud, *then*..." instead of "I'll feel proud *when*..."

TOO LATE TO MAKE A DECISION

Have you ever thought, "It's too late for me"? We hear people say things like, "My ship has sailed. That bell's been rung. It's all over."

Are you ready for some shocking news? However old you are right now is younger than you'll ever be again.

That's not meant to shock you—well, yeah, it actually is because sometimes we need a gentle or slightly rougher kick in the pants to make us realize it's time to make a decision and get going.

I know you could cite a laundry list of evidence that proves all the reasons why it's too late for you to find a mate, start a business, write a book, learn to dance, repair a relationship, or learn to speak Russian. I'm sure you've sat with well-meaning friends or family members who reinforce that thought as a means of support and empathy. But this thought is not a fact, and in fact it's the very thought that prevents you from following through on what your dream is. It literally crushes the seedling of curiosity and the vision of what's possible because you thwart the possibility before it can transform from a thought into a reality.

Is there a reality check that makes something so? Of course you could go to the extreme to prove your point and argue that you are being practical and correct. I often hear things from clients like, "You can't say it's just a thought that I could try out for the Olympic gymnastics team if I'm fifty-five years old."

Even in this exaggerated possibility let's see if that's true. Could you try out? Could you practice gymnastics? Could you compete? Yes, you could do all of those things. Of course you might not achieve the final outcome of being on the team, but who would you have become in the process of this pursuit? At the writing of this book, the forty-six-year-old Olympic gymnast Oksana Chusovitina from Uzbekistan has became the oldest gymnast in history to compete. The 2020 Tokyo Olympics became her eighth Olympic Games.

Rather than asking if it's possible to achieve your dream at your age, the more relevant question to ask yourself is: "Who do I have to become to achieve this goal? Am I willing to be that person? Will I decide no matter what that I will find a way?"

The thought "It's too late for me" can only be true if you're dead. Since you're reading this book, that can't be true. So let's move on!

You can either fight for your limitations or for your limitlessness.

As always, you get to decide.

GET FUTURE-FOCUSED

Imagine for a minute going somewhere in your car. Assuming your car is facing the road, do you put the car in reverse? No! In other words, getting to a new destination presupposes that we aren't going to go backward.

The past is the past. Deciding the future takes place in our minds. We have to be able to imagine future possibilities, and they are only a thought away. You might protest with lots of limiting thoughts and evidence that imagining the future is impossible, but I want you to challenge that thought. Would a million dollars be enough incentive?

THE MILLION-DOLLAR CHALLENGE

Let's take relationships. You might say, "I am too old to find a partner. No one wants a sixty-year-old woman. Men want younger women." You might even find lots of statistical information that proves that. But what's the upside of that thought? Is fighting for your limitations the result you want to create? Let's imagine for a minute I'd pay you $1 million for every story you could find that proved women over sixty found love partners. How much would you earn? I'd bet you'd find hundreds if not thousands of those stories including women in their sixties, seventies, and even eighties finding love with a new partner.

When we drive to our destination by looking in the rearview mirror and keep one foot on the brake by focusing on our limiting thoughts, we decide to give up in advance because we don't see ourselves getting anywhere. You might even protest, "I tried the dating apps! I went out on ten dates with total creeps who only wanted sex,\ or were so boring or had so much baggage, and I gave up." Ten? Really? Twenty? Are you saying you'll give something you value as a deep core desire (e.g., having a loving relationship and partnership) a limited number of tries before you abandon it? Not to mention that every try you make is undoubtedly smudged with the thoughts: "It can't work. Every guy (or woman) is the same. They all want someone younger, richer, thinner, smarter (insert your own bias here). All the good ones are taken."

So how do we get future-focused if our thoughts are telling us it's not even possible? Believe it or not, it doesn't even have to start with a thought; it could start with a feeling. The real reason any of us want anything is because of how we think having it will make us feel.

We think we will feel more loved and secure when we have a relationship. We think we will feel more certain and decisive if we have the predictable financial security of a paying job. We imagine we will feel happier and more confident if we weigh a certain amount and fit into a particular size. All of these thoughts are simply made-up. One person believes that a size 0 would make her happy while another believes that a size 12 would be a dream.

So how is it possible to create a feeling in advance, in the absence of having the thing you want?

When it comes to goals like money, health, and love, we believe if we just had the right amount of money or the perfect body or the best soul mate our lives would be perfect, but the truth is if we don't have those things, we haven't reached the vibrational match required to obtain them. Remember how you have to make a polar bear welcome if you want it to live in Arizona? The same is true if you want a lover, the perfect job, or a healthy, fit body. If you manifest any of those without having transformed yourself, those accomplishments will be short-lived. As Derek Rydall, the man who brought us the polar bear concept, says, "You might be able to manifest a higher paycheck, but you'll just be broke at a higher income level."

We have to create the conditions in our mind that see us as aligned with what we are going toward, and then we need to act as if we are already there. It's a little like the teaching wisdom of Mr. Miyagi in the movie *The Karate Kid*. Mr. Myagi had his young disciple, Daniel, who wanted to learn karate, perform mundane, seemingly unrelated chores like waxing Miyagi's car and painting his house instead of actually teaching Daniel the karate moves he expected. What Daniel perceived as unfair slave labor proved radically different when he was able to instinctively use those moves, which were karate defensive blocks, to protect himself in a fight. In other words, you have to prepare yourself to be the person you think you want that future person to be.

For example, how would you act if you had already met the love of your life? If you think you'd be happier, start *being* happier and acting as if you are happier. You could be happy about other things, not just the lover you don't have, but you could decide to focus on something as simple as being happy about your health, your work, the friends you have in your life, the fact you have electricity and clean water. The truth is when we begin to take inventory of all the things we routinely expect to function without ever deciding to be happy or grateful, we miss a lot of opportunities for happiness. You can activate the feeling of happiness for no reason, no conditions, no circumstance at all. Once you decide to pay attention to what the vibration of happiness feels like in your body, you can learn to recreate that feeling.

In the following story, we see how Sage's curiousity and determination for creating a meaningful life is always at the forefront of her thoughts. She says what drives her most is asking the question, "What's next?

SAGE'S STORY

Funny how I'm in my mid-fifties and still pondering what I want to be when I grow up.

Lately, I've been fascinated with monkeys. All things monkeys. Via the internet, I've educated myself on the various species of this humanlike animal, their mannerisms and characteristic traits. In a childlike curiosity, I want to hold one. I want to have one. Yes, I'm fully aware of the "throwing of the poop"; nonetheless, I'm all in. This obsession has me contemplating returning to school to study primatology. But is there time?

In my late forties, following a stroke and sudden renal failure that ultimately resulted in my current regime of dialysis treatments three times per week at three hours each session while waiting patiently for a kidney transplant, I learned to swim. Yes, I had my very first swim lesson when I was almost fifty. I was actually terrified of the water because I didn't know how to swim, but I consciously decided that as soon as I got the port out of my chest, the one that was inserted so I could receive dialysis and the one that prevented me from taking a bath or immersing myself in water for over a year, no matter what fear or terror I had, I would immerse my entire being in the water. Dialysis is and was a very demanding, uncomfortable, and severely restrictive experience, but it led to my fervent passion for swimming. Water has been healing for me. I feel buoyantly limitless in the water as though I possess superhuman powers and strength.

Ironically my extreme health crises didn't bring up the same "Is there enough time?" concerns that thinking about my birdies leaving the nest does. I feel like there is so much more I need to teach my son and daughter. Will they remember all the life lessons we've taught them without me helicoptering over them as their fearlessly observant momma?

I try not to think too much about my children leaving as this inevitable reality makes me feel quietly anxious. I secretly wonder if I'm projecting worry about them because I'm really worried about myself. My critical voice has often left me judging and doubting my own parenting abilities.

But something profound happens when I shift my thoughts to notice what is true: My husband and I have done our best. There is no denying my children are fully prepared. They are capable. They will make mistakes just like we did, and they will find their way. I notice these empowered thoughts make me feel certain. I feel optimistic when I focus on believing they can and should make their own decisions, follow their dreams, and embark upon additional ones. These feelings of certainty and optimism buoy me like the water, encouraging me to more freely explore my own interests and follow my impulses. As long as I am living, I get to decide who and what I want to be. As I continually grow (up), I discover even more of myself, and that is a worthy exploration. Is there enough time? Yes, there is time. Time to live. Time to be. Time to adapt like water to whatever form of life I create. And yes, time is fleeting, so the time is NOW.

* * * *

At the writing of this book Sage received the kidney transplant she had been awaiting for ten years. Not only will she earn back the twelve hours of time she devoted weekly to dialysis, but the new kidney has shown promises of increasing her overall wellness, energy, and stamina. With this new gift of extra time, I can't wait to see what she creates!

THOUGHT GEM

JUST DECIDE you are the author of your life and now is your time to write your future stories.

KEEP THE JOURNEY GOING

CLOSING THOUGHTS

So you've arrived at the end of this book, but really at the beginning of a new chapter in your life: the chapter where you are the author. You are poised to design your life by deliberate decision, not by default, and you've had some great practice along the way. (You did do the workbook exercises, didn't you?)

We all know the story of Pandora's box, where curiosity resulted in Pandora unleashing a world of problems that did not exist. But I believe curiosity will actually open your *panoramic* box, the one that enables you to see a full and wide view of everything with clarity. Yes, let curiosity be your guide for dreaming and imagining the best-case scenario of what is possible when you are willing to make decisions.

The question before you now is *deciding* what you will do with this newfound wealth of information. WIll you literally slide this book to the shelf or make sure that it is actively used as a tool for self-help?

Why did you pick up this book? What did you want to learn to do or stop doing?

At the beginning of this book I promised if you stuck with me to the end, you'd learn that making decisions meant you could have your own back and relinquish the need to please others at your own expense. I promised you'd gain the tools to manage your thoughts and grow into true emotional adulthood. I promised you'd gain confidence when making decisions and consequently up-level every area of your life from your relationships to your health and your career.

So ask yourself, "What have I done to start pivoting or launching my thoughts in this direction?" Remember, this is a journey that starts with thoughts, and it is a journey about becoming that person who is in charge of her thoughts. Are you acknowledging and appreciating your progress?

Remember, I also cautioned you to never use awareness as a weapon against yourself, so wherever you are at this moment is exactly right. You can only ever be where you are, but staying there is entirely your choice. I promised you could decide to be more authentic and live in greater alignment in order to regret-proof your life.

You've learned that your past doesn't create your future, but your thoughts create everything. Your real secret power lies squarely between your ears in that beautiful brain of yours.

It's been an honor to share this journey and hold the space for you while you decided you were ready to believe in yourself.

All along I knew you held that power within you.

So, friend, tell me, how did you JUST DECIDE to spend those precious 86,400 seconds a day?

XO, *Tsgoyna*

Thank You
for trusting me and allowing me
to be a part of your journey.

&

ONE LAST THING...

Your feedback means a lot.
I'd love to hear about your wins and challenges
so I can make the next book even better.
Contact me at:
justdecidecoach@gmail.com

If you found this helpful
please write a review
on Amazon.

Your review will help others!

Thank You
tsgoyna, xo

5/25

Made in the USA
Middletown, DE
20 March 2022

62957051R00086